IN THE KITCHEN

ROSEMARY MOON

Good Books

The NSPCC works to protect children from abuse and neglect through its network of Child Protection Teams in England, Wales and Northern Ireland, and via its Child Protection Helpline. In 1991, the Society helped more than 50,000 children at risk.

Produced for CPC (United Kingdom) Ltd by Good Books (GB Publications Limited), Lagard Farm, Whitley, Wilts SN12 8RL

ISBN 0 946555 24 9 *(softcover)*
0 946555 25 7 *(hardcover)*

Photography: Nick Carman
Food stylist: Janice Murfitt
Editor: Ros Tarrant
Design and typesetting: Baseline Creative, Bath
Illustrations: Fiona Cowman
Art director: Lorrie Mack
Stylist: Maria Jacques

Colour separation by Fotographics Ltd, London and Hong Kong

Made and printed in Great Britain by Butler & Tanner Ltd, Frome

For further information about MARMITE yeast extract, write to CPC (UK) Ltd, Esher, Surrey KT10 9PN

CONTENTS

INTRODUCTION

Rosemary Moon is a regular cookery presenter on BBC Television, and gives talks and demonstrations all round the country. Among the books she has written are *The Mainly Microwave Cookbook, The Combination Oven Cookbook* (with Val Collins) and *Delicatessen - a Celebration and Cookbook.*

"I really was a MARMITE baby. I've always loved MARMITE and was delighted to be asked to write this book. I hope you will enjoy trying the recipes as much as I've enjoyed creating them. Happy Cooking!"

MARMITE yeast extract has been a family favourite for several generations. Many of us were introduced to 'MARMITE SOLDIERS' as one of our first solid foods, and have been enjoying the product's unique savoury taste ever since.

MARMITE was first produced in this country at the end of the last century. Because of its nutritional benefits it was originally sold through clinics and welfare organisations to mothers with young children. Today, as then, it is recognised that MARMITE yeast extract makes a valuable contribution to the diet of the young.

MARMITE is made from yeast, one of the richest natural sources of B group vitamins (each 4g serving provides 16.6% of the recommended daily amount of five B group vitamins). It is a reliable source of folic acid - an important vitamin for women during pregnancy, and for women who are thinking of becoming pregnant.

MARMITE is delicious spread thinly on bread or toast. Add a thin layer of MARMITE yeast extract to your favourite sandwich combination and it will give it an extra savoury 'bite', without overpowering the other flavours. When cooking, a spoonful of MARMITE enriches the taste.

All the recipes in the book have been specially created by Rosemary Moon, using MARMITE as an ingredient. The range of recipes, from soups and starters to children's party food, demonstrates how versatile an ingredient MARMITE is - a real 'mate' in the kitchen.

NOTES

■ Quantities for ingredients are given in both metric and Imperial measures, with the figures rounded up or down to provide a practical working quantity. As they are not interchangeable, always follow one set of measurements only. (See conversion tables and oven temperatures below.)

■ The microwave recipes have been tested in a 700W microwave cooker. Those with a lower wattage oven should refer to the chart below. The times given are approximate, so make sure you check the food regularly while it is cooking.

■ The number of servings per recipe is based on an average appetite. Adjustments should be made for those with light or large appetites.

■ Cooking margarine can be substituted for butter in those recipes that use it.

■ Wherever possible use fresh herbs. If unavailable, substitute the dried equivalent as instructed in the recipe.

■ All eggs are size 3 unless otherwise stated.

■ Spoon measures are level unless otherwise stated.

■ The **V** symbol denotes vegetarian recipes.

CONVERSION TABLES

WEIGHT CONVERSIONS

IMPERIAL	METRIC
1/2 OZ	15G
1 OZ	25G
2 OZ	50G
3 OZ	75G
4 OZ	125G
5 OZ	150G
6 OZ	175G
7 OZ	200G
8 OZ	225G
9 OZ	250G
10 OZ	275G
11 OZ	300G
12 OZ	350G
13 OZ	375G
14 OZ	400G
15 OZ	425G
16 OZ (1 LB)	450G

EXACT CONVERSION 1 OZ = 28.3495G

LIQUID CONVERSIONS

IMPERIAL	METRIC
1 FL OZ	25ML
2 FL OZ	50ML
3 FL OZ	75ML
4 FL OZ	100ML
5 FL OZ/1/4 PINT	150ML
10 FL OZ/1/2 PINT	300ML
15 FL OZ/3/4 PINT	450ML
20 FL OZ/1 PINT	575ML

1 TABLESPOON = 15ML

MICROWAVE

USE THIS CHART TO ADJUST COOKING TIMES FOR LOWER WATTAGE OVENS.

650/700 WATT	600 WATT	500 WATT
30 SEC	35 SEC	40 SEC
1 MIN	1 MIN 10	1 MIN 20
2 MIN	2 MIN 30	3 MIN
3 MIN	3 MIN 30	4 MIN
4 MIN	4 MIN 30	5 MIN
5 MIN	6 MIN	6 MIN 30
10 MIN	11 MIN 30	13 MIN
15 MIN	17 MIN	20 MIN
20 MIN	23 MIN	26 MIN
30 MIN	35 MIN	39 MIN

OVEN TEMPERATURES

°C	°F	GAS MARK
110	225	1/4
130	250	1/2
140	275	1
150	300	2
160	325	3
180	350	4
190	375	5
200	400	6
220	425	7
230	450	8
240	475	9

LEFT Spring Onion Cheesecake   RIGHT Bombay Bites with Spicy Tomato Sauce   BOTTOM Celery and Stilton Soup

CELERY AND STILTON SOUP

Preparation time: 10 minutes
Cooking time: 30 minutes

1 LARGE ONION, CHOPPED
1 HEAD OF CELERY, TRIMMED AND SLICED
1 TBSP (3 TSP) **MARMITE** YEAST EXTRACT
900ML (1 1/2 PINTS) BOILING WATER
1 TBSP CHOPPED FRESH THYME (OR 1 TSP DRIED)
4-5 LEAVES LOVAGE, CHOPPED (OPTIONAL)
125G (4OZ) STILTON CHEESE, CRUMBLED
SALT AND FRESHLY GROUND BLACK PEPPER
45ML (3 TBSP) SINGLE CREAM OR CRÈME FRAÎCHE
INNER LEAVES OF CELERY FOR GARNISH

1. Place the onion and celery in a large saucepan. Dissolve the MARMITE in the boiling water and add to the pan with the thyme and lovage. Simmer, covered, for 30 minutes.

2. Liquidise or process the soup until smooth, then add the cheese and blend again. Season to taste.

3. Reheat the soup gently if necessary and stir in the cream or crème fraîche just before serving. Garnish with celery leaves.

Serves 4-6

Lovage is easy to grow in the garden - but it gets about 2 metres high, so put it at the back of the bed! It has a strong, peppered, celery flavour and also goes very well with pumpkin.

OATMEAL SOUP

This variation on a favourite Scottish recipe is cheap to make but has a real taste of luxury.

Preparation time: 10 minutes
Cooking time: 35 minutes

25G (1OZ) BUTTER OR MARGARINE
1 LARGE ONION, FINELY CHOPPED
50G (2OZ) MEDIUM OATMEAL
2 TSP **MARMITE** YEAST EXTRACT
575ML (1 PINT) BOILING WATER
300ML (1/2 PINT) MILK
SALT AND LEMON PEPPER
1 TBSP CHOPPED FRESH PARSLEY
150ML (1/4 PINT) SINGLE CREAM (OPTIONAL)

1. Melt the butter or margarine in a large saucepan, add the onion and cook slowly until softened but not brown. Add the oatmeal and cook for a few seconds.

2. Dissolve the MARMITE in the boiling water and add to the pan. Bring to the boil, stirring constantly, then cover and simmer slowly for 30 minutes. Stir the soup from time to time.

3. Add the milk to the soup, then blend until smooth in a liquidiser or food processor. Season to taste with salt and lemon pepper and add the parsley.

4. Reheat the soup if necessary. Add the cream just before serving.

Serves 4

Lemon pepper adds a slight sharpness to this soup. If it is not available, add a little freshly grated lemon zest.

BOMBAY BITES WITH SPICY TOMATO SAUCE

These are good for a starter or for cocktail nibbles.

Preparation time: 20 minutes
Cooking time: 20-25 minutes

SPICY TOMATO SAUCE:
1 ONION, FINELY CHOPPED
2TBSP VEGETABLE OIL
1TSP MARMITE YEAST EXTRACT
1TSP GROUND GINGER
1TSP GROUND CUMIN
400G (14OZ) CAN CHOPPED TOMATOES
SALT AND FRESHLY GROUND BLACK PEPPER
CHILLI OR HOT PEPPER SAUCE, TO TASTE

BOMBAY BITES:
75G (3OZ) WHOLEWHEAT BREADCRUMBS
1 ONION, VERY FINELY CHOPPED
2 CLOVES GARLIC, CRUSHED
400G (14OZ) CAN CHICK PEAS, DRAINED
2TSP MARMITE YEAST EXTRACT
SALT AND FRESHLY GROUND BLACK PEPPER

VEGETABLE OIL FOR FRYING

1. To prepare the sauce, cook the onion in the oil with the MARMITE, ginger and cumin until soft. Add the tomatoes, season, and cook for 15-20 minutes. Add chilli or hot pepper sauce to taste, and adjust seasoning.

2. Mix together all the ingredients for the bites in a liquidiser or food processor. Shape the mixture into 16-18 bite-sized balls.

3. Shallow fry the bites for 2-3 minutes on each side, until lightly browned. Serve them, hot or cold, with the sauce.

Serves 4-6

IF YOU DO NOT HAVE A GARLIC PRESS ADD A LITTLE SALT TO A GARLIC CLOVE, THEN CHOP ROUGHLY AND MASH TO A PASTE WITH THE FLAT BLADE OF A KNIFE. THE SALT DRAWS OUT MOISTURE AND MAKES THE JOB EASY.

SPRING ONION CHEESECAKE

This unusual dish is a delicious cross between a quiche and a soufflé, baked in a hot-water pastry crust.

Preparation time: 30 minutes
Cooking time: 1 hour 45 minutes
Cooling time: 1 hour

PASTRY:
125G (4OZ) PLAIN FLOUR
1TSP MARMITE YEAST EXTRACT
6TBSP WATER
25G (1OZ) SOLID SUNFLOWER FAT OR LARD

FILLING:
125G (4OZ) STREAKY BACON, CHOPPED
400G (14OZ) CREAM CHEESE
1TBSP (3TSP) MARMITE YEAST EXTRACT
3 EGGS, SEPARATED
25G (1OZ) PLAIN FLOUR
1 BUNCH SPRING ONIONS, TRIMMED AND SLICED
125G (4OZ) FROMAGE FRAIS
SALT AND FRESHLY GROUND BLACK PEPPER
CHOPPED SPRING ONIONS TO GARNISH

Preheat oven to 160°C (325°F/gas mark 3)

1. To prepare the pastry, place the flour in a bowl and the remaining ingredients in a small saucepan. Bring the water to the boil to melt the fat. Pour the liquid into the flour and mix well, pinching together with your hand to form the pastry into a ball.

2. Knead lightly on a floured surface and roll out into a circle. Use to line a deep, 20cm (8in) loose-bottomed flan tin, pushing the pastry up the sides with your fingers. Chill until required.

3. Cook the bacon, but do not crisp it. Remove from the pan with a slotted spoon and allow to cool. In a large bowl, beat the cream cheese with the MARMITE, then add the egg yolks with the remaining ingredients, including the bacon. Whisk the egg whites until stiff, then fold into the mixture.

4. Spoon the filling into the prepared pastry case and smooth the top. Bake for about 1 hour 45 minutes, until firm, set and browned. Turn the oven off, open the door and leave for 1 hour.

5. Serve warm or chilled. Garnish with a few freshly chopped spring onions.

Serves 8

QUORN SALADE TIÈDE

Warm salads are very popular and an excellent way to start a dinner party. Quorn is a pure vegetable protein that marinates well and can quickly be stir-fried and tossed into a prepared salad just before serving.

Preparation time: 30 minutes to marinate
15 minutes to prepare the salad
Cooking time: 5 minutes

MARINADE:
2 TBSP ORANGE JUICE
1 TBSP OLIVE OIL
1 TSP MARMITE YEAST EXTRACT
1 TSP CHOPPED FRESH TARRAGON
(OR ½ TSP DRIED)
1 TSP DEMERARA SUGAR
250G (9OZ) QUORN

1 LOLLO ROSSO LETTUCE
1 BUNCH WATERCRESS
½ SMALL CUCUMBER, DICED
10-12 RADISHES, TRIMMED AND QUARTERED
2 TOMATOES, QUARTERED
1 HEAD CHICORY, TRIMMED AND DIVIDED INTO LEAVES
2 STALKS CELERY, CHOPPED
1 ORANGE, PEELED AND CUT INTO SEGMENTS
2 TBSP OLIVE OIL FOR FRYING
ZEST OF THE ORANGE FOR GARNISH

1. Mix together the first five ingredients for the marinade, add the Quorn and stir carefully. Cover and leave for 30 minutes, stirring once or twice.

2. Break the lettuce and watercress into bite-sized pieces, and place in a salad bowl. Add the remaining salad items and orange segments.

3. Heat the oil in a frying pan, add the Quorn and marinade and stir-fry quickly for 4-5 minutes. Add to the salad (any oil will act as a salad dressing), garnish with the orange zest and serve immediately.

Serves 6

Arrange the salad on individual plates in advance. That way you can make sure that everyone has some of all the ingredients.

As an alternative to Quorn, you can use diced breast of chicken and adjust cooking time accordingly.

PRAWN PROFITEROLES

Preparation time: 40 minutes
Cooking time: 45 minutes
Cooling time: 1 hour

CHOUX PASTRY:
50G (2OZ) BUTTER
150ML (¼ PINT) WATER
65G (2½OZ) STRONG PLAIN FLOUR, SIEVED
2 EGGS, BEATEN

FILLING:
1 SMALL ONION, FINELY CHOPPED
1 CLOVE GARLIC, CRUSHED
25G (1OZ) BUTTER
½ TSP MARMITE YEAST EXTRACT
GRATED ZEST OF A LEMON
200G (7OZ) CAN CHOPPED TOMATOES
175G (6OZ) PEELED PRAWNS

SAUCE:
6 TBSP THICK NATURAL YOGURT
JUICE OF 1 LEMON
2 TBSP CHOPPED FRESH PARSLEY
SALT AND FRESHLY GROUND BLACK PEPPER

Preheat oven to 220°C (425°F/gas mark 7)

1. Lightly grease a large baking sheet.

2. To make the pastry, place the butter and water in a saucepan and bring to a rolling boil, making certain that the butter has melted. Shoot in the flour and beat vigorously, off the heat, until the pastry forms a ball and leaves the sides of the pan. Cool slightly, then gradually beat in the eggs to give a smooth paste that will hold its shape.

3. Form the mixture into 12 small mounds on the baking sheet, using two teaspoons. Bake for 20 minutes. Remove the profiteroles, slit the sides with a sharp knife and return to the oven for a further 25-30 minutes at 180°C (350°F/gas mark 4), until browned and crisp. Cool on a wire rack.

4. To prepare the filling, cook the onion and garlic in the butter until soft. Add the MARMITE, lemon zest and tomatoes and cook for 10 minutes, or until slightly reduced and thickened. Cool completely, then stir in the prawns.

5. Make the sauce by mixing all the ingredients together. Season to taste.

6. Put a little filling inside each profiterole. Top with a little of the yogurt sauce just before serving.

Serves 4

TOP Vegetable Terrine   BOTTOM Quorn Salade Tiède

TOP Prawn Profiteroles BOTTOM Summer Soup

SUMMER SOUP

This refreshing chilled soup has a strong and savoury flavour.

Preparation time: 5 minutes
Cooking time: 25 minutes
Chilling time: 2 hours

1 LARGE ONION, SLICED
25G (1OZ) BUTTER OR MARGARINE
175G (6OZ) WATERCRESS
225G (8OZ) FROZEN OR
PREPARED FRESH SPINACH
1 TBSP (3 TSP) **MARMITE** YEAST EXTRACT
575ML (1 PINT) BOILING WATER
2 TBSP CHOPPED FRESH MINT (OR 2 TSP DRIED)
300ML (1/2 PINT) MILK
45-60ML (3-4 TBSP) FROMAGE FRAIS
SALT AND FRESHLY GROUND BLACK PEPPER

1. In a large saucepan, cook the onion in the butter or margarine until soft. Add the watercress and spinach.

2. Dissolve the MARMITE in the boiling water and add to the pan with the mint. Bring to the boil, cover and simmer for 10-15 minutes.

3. Blend the soup until smooth in a liquidiser or food processor. Allow to cool, then chill for at least 2 hours.

4. Whisk the milk and fromage frais, and add to the soup. Season to taste and add crushed ice to chill further when serving.

Serves 6

THINLY SPREAD **MARMITE** YEAST EXTRACT ON BREAD AND TOAST TO MAKE CROUTONS TO SERVE WITH SOUP.

VEGETABLE PURÉES ARE OFTEN MORE INTERESTING THAN THE VEGETABLE IN ITS ORIGINAL FORM. EXPERIMENT WITH TASTE COMBINATIONS. TRY: CELERIAC PURÉE MIXED WITH MASHED POTATO; A PURÉE OF PEAS MIXED WITH GENTLY COOKED ONION, GARLIC, MINT AND A LITTLE SUGAR; CARROT PURÉE WITH ADDED PEPPER, A PINCH OF SUGAR AND A TOUCH OF GINGER.

VEGETABLE TERRINE

Preparation time: 40 minutes
Chilling time: 2-3 hours

450G (1LB) POTATOES, PEELED AND CUT INTO PIECES
350G (12OZ) LEEKS, TRIMMED AND SLICED
25G (1OZ) BUTTER OR MARGARINE
1 TSP **MARMITE** YEAST EXTRACT
SALT AND FRESHLY GROUND BLACK PEPPER
450G (1LB) CARROTS, PEELED AND SLICED
125G (4OZ) CHEDDAR CHEESE, GRATED
450G (1LB) PARSNIPS,
PEELED AND COARSELY SHREDDED
200G (7OZ) CREAM CHEESE
1/2 TSP GROUND NUTMEG
1 TSP DEMERARA SUGAR
CHOPPED FRESH PARSLEY TO GARNISH
TOAST OR CRACKERS FOR SERVING

1. Boil the potatoes with the leeks until just cooked. Drain very thoroughly. Place in a liquidiser or food processor with the butter or margarine and MARMITE, and blend to a smooth, thick purée. Season to taste.

2. Line a 675g (1½lb) loaf tin with non-stick greaseproof paper. Place the purée in a layer in the bottom of the tin.

3. Cook the carrots until just tender. Drain thoroughly and place in a liquidiser or food processor with the cheese. Blend to a thick purée, then season with black pepper. Spoon into the loaf tin, making a layer over the potato.

4. Cook the parsnips for 5 minutes. Meanwhile, in a bowl, beat the cream cheese until smooth with the nutmeg and demerara sugar, then mix in the drained parsnips. Spoon into the tin, over the previous layers.

5. Allow to cool, then chill for 2-3 hours. Turn out onto a serving plate and remove the non-stick paper.

6. Garnish with chopped parsley, then serve with freshly made toast or crackers.

Serves 6

It is a good idea to prepare all the layers before you assemble the terrine. Try to keep them all fairly stiff and dry. If the potato and leek purée is a little wet, put the carrot layer in the tin first and the potato in the centre.

STUFFED PEARS

This recipe works just as well with avocados or ripe William pears. The stuffing is seasoned cottage cheese, so it is neither too filling nor too fattening - especially if dessert pears are used.

Preparation time: 10 minutes

2 LARGE AVOCADOS OR 4 RIPE WILLIAM PEARS
RAW SPINACH OR LOLLO ROSSO LETTUCE
FOR SERVING
225G (8OZ) COTTAGE CHEESE,
THE FLAVOUR OF YOUR CHOICE
1/2TSP **MARMITE** YEAST EXTRACT
1TSP HOT PEPPER SAUCE (OPTIONAL)
1TSP CHOPPED FRESH PARSLEY
25G (1OZ) TOASTED ALMONDS, CHOPPED
PAPRIKA

1. Remove the stones from the avocados or halve and core the William pears, making a well to receive the stuffing. Place the prepared pears in individual dishes, on a bed of raw spinach or lollo rosso.

2. Mix together the cottage cheese, MARMITE and pepper sauce, then add the parsley. Spoon the cheese into the pears.

3. Scatter the almonds over the pears and garnish with a little paprika. Serve immediately.

Serves 4

Cottage cheese with added fruit such as mango and apricot works particularly well with this recipe.

CRUNCHY VEGETABLE ROLLS

These are a variation on the popular Spring Rolls and are made using filo pastry instead of pancakes. Baked in the oven, they are much healthier than the traditional fried rolls.

Preparation time: 25 minutes
Cooking time: 15 minutes

1 TBSP SESAME OIL
1 TBSP SOY SAUCE
1 TSP **MARMITE** YEAST EXTRACT
PINCH 5-SPICE POWDER
1 SMALL RED PEPPER,
DE-SEEDED AND CUT INTO STRIPS
6 RADISHES, SLICED
4CM (1 1/2IN) PIECE FRESH GINGER,
PEELED AND GRATED
1 BUNCH SPRING ONIONS,
TRIMMED AND CHOPPED
50G (2OZ) BEANSPROUTS
227G (8OZ) CAN SLICED BAMBOO SHOOTS,
DRAINED
12 SMALL SHEETS FILO PASTRY
50-75ML (2-3FL OZ) VEGETABLE OIL FOR
BRUSHING
SALAD OR RAW VEGETABLE GARNISH
SOY OR SATAY SAUCE FOR SERVING

Preheat oven to 220°C (425°F/gas mark 7)

1. Mix together the sesame oil, soy sauce, MARMITE and 5-spice powder in a large bowl. Stir in next six ingredients and leave for 5 minutes.

2. Brush each sheet of filo with oil and fold in half to form a square. Divide the filling between the 12 sheets, placing it bottom centre of each sheet. Oil the exposed pastry, then fold the sides in, over the vegetables, and roll into parcels. Place on a lightly greased baking sheet and brush with a little oil.

3. Bake for 15 minutes. Serve immediately with a salad or raw vegetable garnish and a little soy or satay sauce.

Makes 12, serves 4-6

Don't be too generous with the filling, otherwise the pastry will split when you fold it.

SOME OF THE MORE UNUSUAL SALAD LEAVES NOW AVAILABLE, SUCH AS FEUILLE DE CHÊNE (OAK LEAF), THE FRILLY RED-TIPPED LOLLO ROSSO OR THE ALL-GREEN LOLLO BLONDO, TEND TO WILT RATHER QUICKLY. THEY WILL REVIVE IF YOU LEAVE THEM FOR A WHILE STANDING IN ICED WATER.

MIX A LITTLE **MARMITE** YEAST EXTRACT WITH BOILING WATER TO USE AS A GLAZE FOR SAVOURY VEGAN PIES.

Top Chestnut Casserole   Bottom Peasants' Pot

MAIN MEALS

ALABAMA BEANS

Preparation time: 10 minutes
(plus 8 hours or overnight soaking for beans)
Cooking time: 45 minutes

375G (13OZ) BLACK-EYE OR HARICOT BEANS,
SOAKED AND DRAINED
2 TBSP VEGETABLE OIL
1 LARGE ONION, FINELY CHOPPED
1 TBSP DARK MUSCOVADO SUGAR
2 TBSP TOMATO KETCHUP
2 TSP DRY MUSTARD POWDER
2 TSP WORCESTERSHIRE SAUCE
1 TBSP (3 TSP) MARMITE YEAST EXTRACT
575ML (1 PINT) BOILING WATER
225G (8OZ) SPICY SAUSAGE, THICKLY SLICED
(OPTIONAL)
FRESHLY GROUND BLACK PEPPER
1 TBSP CHOPPED FRESH PARSLEY

1. Heat the oil in a large saucepan, add the onion and cook gently until soft.

2. Stir the sugar, ketchup, mustard and Worcestershire sauce into the pan. Dissolve the MARMITE in the boiling water and add to the pan with the beans. Stir well.

3. Bring to the boil, then cover and simmer for 30 minutes or until the beans are soft. Remove the lid halfway through cooking to allow sauce to thicken. If using sausage, add to the pan for the last 10-15 minutes.

4. Season to taste with pepper and add the parsley. Serve with a green salad or green vegetables.

Serves 4

(without meat option)

CHESTNUT CASSEROLE

Dried chestnuts are available in most health food shops and make an unusual and filling casserole.

Preparation time: 15 minutes
(plus overnight soaking for chestnuts)
Cooking time: 45-60 minutes

225G (8OZ) DRIED CHESTNUTS, SOAKED AND DRAINED
2 TBSP VEGETABLE OIL
1 LARGE LEEK, TRIMMED AND SLICED
1 GREEN PEPPER, DE-SEEDED AND CUT INTO STRIPS
2 LARGE CARROTS, CUT INTO MATCHSTICKS
3 STICKS CELERY, SLICED
1 GREEN CHILLI, FINELY CHOPPED (OPTIONAL)
5CM (2IN) PIECE FRESH GINGER, PEELED AND GRATED
2 TBSP WHOLEMEAL FLOUR
1 TBSP (3 TSP) MARMITE YEAST EXTRACT
575ML (1 PINT) BOILING WATER
FEW BLADES MACE
2 BAY LEAVES
SALT AND FRESHLY GROUND BLACK PEPPER
CHOPPED FRESH PARSLEY TO GARNISH

Preheat oven to 180°C (350°F/gas mark 4)

1. Heat the oil in a large flameproof casserole and cook all the vegetables with the chilli and ginger, until soft.

2. Stir in the flour and cook for a few seconds. Dissolve the MARMITE in the boiling water and add gradually to the pan. Bring to the boil, stirring constantly. Add the mace, bay leaves and chestnuts.

3. Transfer to the oven and cook, covered, for 45-60 minutes, until the chestnuts are tender. Adjust seasoning and garnish with parsley before serving.

Serves 4

PEASANTS' POT

This is a good recipe for mid-week entertaining or an informal weekend party. It can easily be prepared a day in advance and kept chilled.

Preparation time: 25 minutes
(plus overnight soaking for beans)
Cooking time: 1½-2 hours

450G (1LB) DRIED MIXED BEANS,
SOAKED AND DRAINED
2 LARGE ONIONS, FINELY SLICED
2 TBSP VEGETABLE OIL
675G (1½LB) MIXED ROOT VEGETABLES,
CHOPPED OR SLICED
1 GREEN PEPPER, DE-SEEDED AND CHOPPED
2 X 400G (14OZ) CANS CHOPPED TOMATOES
2 TSP TOMATO PURÉE
1 TBSP (3TSP) MARMITE YEAST EXTRACT
300ML (½ PINT) BOILING WATER
SALT AND FRESHLY GROUND BLACK PEPPER
2 TBSP CHOPPED FRESH MIXED HERBS
(OR 2 TSP DRIED)
3 BAY LEAVES

Preheat oven to 180°C (350°F/gas mark 4)

1. Rinse the drained beans, then place in a saucepan and cover with fresh water. Bring to the boil and cook rapidly for 10 minutes. Continue to simmer the beans until needed.

2. In a very large flameproof casserole dish, cook the onions in the oil, over a low heat, until soft. Add the root vegetables and green pepper, and cook until soft.

3. Drain the beans and add to the pan with the tomatoes and tomato purée. Dissolve the MARMITE in the boiling water and add to the pan to cover all the ingredients, then season with salt, pepper and the herbs.

4. Bring to the boil, then cover. Transfer to the oven and cook for 1½-2 hours, until the beans are soft. Season to taste, and serve with garlic bread.

Serves 6-8

MUSHROOM AND CASHEW RISOTTO

This risotto uses coriander seeds and leaves for an interesting, spicy flavour.

Preparation time: 15 minutes
Cooking time: 30 minutes

2 TBSP VEGETABLE OIL
1 LARGE ONION, FINELY SLICED
1 GREEN PEPPER,
DE-SEEDED AND CUT INTO STRIPS
1 TBSP CORIANDER SEEDS, CRUSHED
1 BAY LEAF
5CM (2IN) PIECE FRESH GINGER,
PEELED AND GRATED
375G (13OZ) BROWN RICE
2 TBSP PEANUT BUTTER
1 TBSP (3TSP) MARMITE YEAST EXTRACT
900ML (1½ PINTS) BOILING WATER
450G (1LB) CUP MUSHROOMS, THICKLY SLICED
2 CLOVES GARLIC, CRUSHED
90G (3½OZ) ROASTED CASHEW NUTS
FRESHLY GROUND BLACK PEPPER
2 TBSP CHOPPED FRESH CORIANDER

1. Heat the oil in a large pan, add the onion, pepper, coriander seeds, bay leaf and ginger, and cook slowly for 5 minutes.

2. Stir the rice into the pan, add the peanut butter and mix well. Dissolve the MARMITE in the boiling water and add it to the pan with half the mushrooms.

3. Bring to the boil. Stir, cover and simmer for 20 minutes.

4. Add the remaining mushrooms, garlic and cashews and cook for a further 5 minutes, uncovered.

5. Season to taste with pepper, then stir half the chopped coriander into the risotto and garnish with the remainder. Serve with a crisp salad.

Serves 4

DRIED RED KIDNEY BEANS ARE POISONOUS UNLESS THEY ARE BOILED RAPIDLY FOR AT LEAST 10 MINUTES AT THE START OF THEIR COOKING TIME.

MUSHROOMS ARE AT THEIR PEAK OF QUALITY FOR ONLY A COUPLE OF DAYS. YOU WILL FREQUENTLY SEE THEM BEING SOLD OFF CHEAPLY BY THE BASKETFUL. THESE BARGAINS MAY BE PAST THEIR PEAK BUT STILL IN A GOOD ENOUGH CONDITION FOR ECONOMICAL SOUPS AND PÂTÉS.

CARBONNADE OF BEEF

This is a traditional French casserole cooked slowly in beer. Serve with boiled or creamed potatoes and plain vegetables in season.

Preparation time: 15 minutes
Cooking time: 4 hours

3 TBSP OLIVE OIL
675G (1½LB) LEAN BRAISING STEAK,
CUT INTO CUBES
125G (4OZ) LEAN BACK BACON, DICED
40G (1½OZ) PLAIN FLOUR
300ML (½ PINT) STOUT OR BITTER BEER
2 TSP MARMITE YEAST EXTRACT
575ML (1 PINT) BOILING WATER
2 TBSP DISTILLED MALT OR WINE VINEGAR
450G (1LB) ONIONS, CHOPPED
BOUQUET GARNI
SALT AND FRESHLY GROUND BLACK PEPPER
1 BAY LEAF
NATURAL YOGURT FOR GARNISH
CHOPPED FRESH CHIVES FOR GARNISH

Preheat oven to 150°C (300°F/gas mark 2)

1. Heat the oil in a large flameproof casserole, add the meat and brown thoroughly to seal in the juices - this will take a good 5-10 minutes. Add the bacon and cook for a further 2-3 minutes; then, using a slotted spoon, remove the meats from the pan.

2. Stir the flour into the juices and brown lightly. Gradually add the beer. Dissolve the MARMITE in the boiling water and add to the pan. Bring to the boil, stirring constantly. Add the vinegar to the sauce.

3. Return the meat to the pan with the onions, bouquet garni, salt, pepper and bay leaf. Bring to the boil, then cover.

4. Transfer to the oven and cook slowly for at least 3½ hours - the longer the better.

5. Adjust seasoning before serving. Garnish with swirls of natural yogurt topped with chives.

Serves 4

SAVOURY CHEESE BURRITOS

You may be able to buy ready-made flour tortillas for this Mexican dish in some supermarkets or delicatessens, though they are simple to make at home. Or you could use ordinary pancakes.

Preparation time: 40 minutes
Cooking time: 30 minutes

TORTILLAS:
450G (1LB) PLAIN FLOUR
75G (3OZ) LARD
1 TBSP (3 TSP) MARMITE YEAST EXTRACT
300ML (½ PINT) BOILING WATER

FILLING:
1 TBSP (3 TSP) MARMITE YEAST EXTRACT
2 x 453G (16OZ) CANS REFRIED BEANS
1 LARGE ONION, FINELY CHOPPED
2 TBSP CHOPPED FRESH CHIVES (OR 2 TSP DRIED)
175G (6OZ) CHEDDAR CHEESE, GRATED

TACO SAUCE TO SERVE

Preheat oven to 200°C (400°F/gas mark 6)

1. To prepare the tortillas, rub the lard into the flour. Dissolve the MARMITE in the boiling water, then add to the flour, mixing to a soft but manageable dough. Add a little extra water if necessary. Turn onto a floured board and knead lightly until smooth.

2. Divide the dough into 12 pieces. Roll each piece into a circle the same diameter as your largest frying pan, then cut the dough into neat circles using a similar sized plate as a guide.

3. Heat the frying pan but do not use any oil. Cook the tortillas for 10 seconds on each side, until they start to look cooked - don't overcook them or they will crack when you fill them. Stack and wrap the cooked tortillas in a clean tea-towel.

4. Beat the second quantity of MARMITE into the refried beans. Place a spoonful of beans in the centre of each tortilla, then top with a little onion, chives and grated cheese. Fold the tortillas into parcels to enclose the filling, then place in a single layer in a roasting tin.

5. Bake for 30 minutes. Serve with taco sauce and a salad of crisp lettuce, tomatoes and avocados.

Serves 4-6

WHOLE BAY LEAVES DO NOT RELEASE ALL THEIR FLAVOUR, SO ALWAYS BREAK THEM BEFORE ADDING TO STEWS AND CASSEROLES.

TOP Chicken Crumble   BOTTOM Savoury Cheese Burritos

Top Carbonnade of Beef   Bottom Spinach and Nut Loaf

CHICKEN CRUMBLE

I like to use chicken thighs on the bone for this crumble, but use boneless if you prefer.

Preparation time: 15 minutes
Cooking time: 1-1¾ hours

1 TSP MARMITE YEAST EXTRACT
30ML (2 TBSP) BOILING WATER
8 CHICKEN THIGHS, BONE IN, SKINNED
2 TBSP VEGETABLE OIL
4 LARGE SALAD ONIONS, SLICED
(OR 1 BUNCH SPRING ONIONS,
TRIMMED AND ROUGHLY CHOPPED)
1 GREEN PEPPER, DE-SEEDED AND SLICED
2 TSP MARMITE YEAST EXTRACT
575ML (1 PINT) BOILING WATER
50G (2OZ) BUTTER OR MARGARINE
225G (8OZ) WHOLEMEAL FLOUR
75G (3OZ) MOZZARELLA CHEESE, GRATED
2 TSP MARMITE YEAST EXTRACT

Preheat oven to 190°C (375°F/gas mark 5)

1. Dissolve 1tsp of MARMITE in the boiling water, then brush the liquid over the chicken. Heat the oil in a large frying pan, then brown the chicken all over. Place the joints in an ovenproof casserole dish, using a slotted spoon.

2. Lightly cook the onions and pepper in the pan, then add to the chicken. Dissolve 2tsp of MARMITE in the second quantity of boiling water and add sufficient of this stock to cover the chicken and vegetables.

3. Cover and cook in the oven for 45-60 minutes, until the chicken is tender.

4. Meanwhile, in a large bowl, prepare the crumble topping. Rub the butter or margarine into the flour, then stir in the Mozzarella and final 2tsp of MARMITE.

5. Drain off a little stock if the casserole dish is very full, reserving it for extra gravy. Spoon the crumble topping over the chicken and return the dish to the oven, uncovered, for a further 20-30 minutes.

Serves 4-6

AN ALTERNATIVE TO COOKING STUFFING INSIDE A CHICKEN IS TO EASE THE STUFFING CAREFULLY BETWEEN THE SKIN AND THE FLESH OF THE BIRD. THIS NOT ONLY HELPS TO KEEP THE BREAST MEAT MOIST, BUT GIVES VERY ATTRACTIVE LOOKING SLICES WHEN CARVED.

SPINACH AND NUT LOAF

This can be eaten hot or cold.

Preparation time: 15 minutes
Cooking time: 1 hour

450G (1LB) FROZEN LEAF SPINACH,
COOKED AND DRAINED
400G (14OZ) MIXED NUTS, FINELY CHOPPED
225G (8OZ) WHOLEWHEAT BREADCRUMBS
1 LARGE ONION, FINELY CHOPPED
1 TBSP TOMATO PURÉE
SALT AND FRESHLY GROUND BLACK PEPPER
1 TSP FRESHLY GRATED NUTMEG
(OR ½ TSP GROUND)
1 TBSP (3 TSP) MARMITE YEAST EXTRACT
2 EGGS, BEATEN
4 RASHERS STREAKY BACON (OPTIONAL)
TOMATOES AND WATERCRESS FOR GARNISH

Preheat oven to 190°C (375°F/gas mark 5)

1. Line a 900g (2lb) loaf tin with non-stick paper.

2. Mix together the spinach, nuts, breadcrumbs, onion, tomato purée and seasonings. Beat the MARMITE with the eggs and use to bind the mixture together.

3. Lay the bacon in diagonal strips along the bottom of the loaf tin and press in the mixture firmly, using the back of a tablespoon. Level the top and cover with foil.

4. Bake in the oven for 1 hour. Turn out onto a serving plate, remove the paper and garnish the loaf with tomatoes and watercress before serving hot. Alternatively, allow the loaf to cool, then chill for 1-2 hours before garnishing and serving.

Serves 6

(without meat option)

NUTS CAN DETERIORATE AND GO RANCID AFTER A WHILE. BOTH WHOLE AND SHELLED NUTS CAN BE FROZEN FOR UP TO A YEAR. IF YOU CHOP OR GRIND THEM FIRST, THEY CAN BE USED STRAIGHT OUT OF THE FREEZER.

IF YOU HAVE OVER-SALTED A SOUP OR STEW, ADD RAW POTATO SLICES. THEY WILL ABSORB SOME OF THE SALT AS THEY COOK. YOU CAN THEN TAKE THEM OUT AND DISCARD THEM.

LAMB EN CROÛTE

Lamb really benefits from the addition of MARMITE to break down any greasiness. In this recipe MARMITE is also used in the pastry for extra flavour. Boned and rolled joints are widely available; leave the meat in its string bag until it is ready to be wrapped in pastry.

Preparation time: 25 minutes
Cooking time: 2-2¹/₂ hours
Cooling time: 1 hour

1.5KG (3¹/₄LB) BONED AND ROLLED JOINT OF
LAMB, LEG OR SHOULDER
1TBSP (3TSP) **MARMITE** YEAST EXTRACT
FRESHLY GROUND BLACK PEPPER

PASTRY:
350G (12OZ) PLAIN FLOUR,
WHOLEWHEAT OR WHITE
75G (3OZ) BUTTER OR MARGARINE
75G (3OZ) SOLID SUNFLOWER FAT OR LARD
2TSP **MARMITE** YEAST EXTRACT
1TBSP CHOPPED FRESH PARSLEY
(OR 1TSP DRIED)
WATER TO MIX

Preheat oven to 220°C (425°F/gas mark 7)

1. Place the lamb on a rack in a roasting tin. Spread the joint with **MARMITE** and season with black pepper. Roast in the oven for 30 minutes, then lower the temperature to 180°C (350°F/gas mark 4) for a further hour, if you like your lamb slightly pink, or 1¹/₂ hours if you like it well done.

2. Remove the lamb and allow to cool for about an hour. Remove the netting from the meat.

3. Heat the oven to 200°C (400°F/gas mark 6). Prepare the pastry. Rub the fats into the flour until the mixture resembles fine breadcrumbs. Stir in the MARMITE and parsley, then add sufficient water to form a firm but manageable dough. Roll out on a floured surface to a rectangle 0.5cm (¹/₄in) thick (no thinner otherwise it will crack), large enough to cover the meat completely. Brush the surface of the pastry with water.

4. Place the joint in the centre of the pastry, enclose it completely and put onto a greased baking sheet, with the pastry joins underneath (make sure the joins are well sealed). Re-roll any trimmings to make decorative leaves etc.

5. Bake for 30-35 minutes, until the pastry is browned and crisp. Carve into slices and serve with gravy and fresh vegetables.

Serves 6-8

BULGAR PILAFF

Bulgar (or bulghur) wheat is a staple ingredient in many Eastern Mediterranean and North African dishes. It is also often used for salads. It cooks well and retains a lovely nutty flavour and texture.

Preparation time: 15 minutes
Cooking time: 20-25 minutes

2 LARGE ONIONS, SLICED
2TBSP VEGETABLE OIL
3 CARROTS, CUT INTO MATCHSTICKS
1 GREEN PEPPER,
DE-SEEDED AND CUT INTO STRIPS
1 RED PEPPER, DE-SEEDED AND CUT INTO STRIPS
2 COURGETTES, CHOPPED
225G (8OZ) BULGAR WHEAT
2TSP **MARMITE** YEAST EXTRACT
575ML (1 PINT) BOILING WATER
SALT AND FRESHLY GROUND BLACK PEPPER
75G (3OZ) NATURALLY ROASTED PEANUTS OR
PINE KERNELS
2TBSP POPPY SEEDS
2 CLOVES GARLIC, CRUSHED
1 BUNCH SPRING ONIONS, FINELY SLICED
1TBSP CHOPPED FRESH CORIANDER OR PARSLEY
GRATED ZEST OF A LEMON (OPTIONAL)

1. In a large pan, cook the onions in the oil until soft. Add the remaining vegetables and cook for 2-3 minutes.

2. Stir the bulgar into the vegetables and heat for a few seconds until it becomes transparent.

3. Dissolve the MARMITE in the boiling water and add to the pan. Bring to the boil, then cover and simmer for 20 minutes until all the liquid is absorbed. Leave to stand, covered, for 2-3 minutes.

4. Season to taste, then stir the remaining ingredients into the pilaff. Serve with a little salad garnish.

Serves 4

If a less strong garlic flavour is preferred, add the garlic with the prepared vegetables.

ADDING **MARMITE** YEAST EXTRACT TO SHORT-CRUST PASTRY
GIVES A SAVOURY CRUST TO PIES, QUICHES AND PASTIES,
WITH A LIGHT, SHORT TEXTURE.

TOP Bulgar Pilaff   *CENTRE Millet and Mushroom Bake*   *BOTTOM Vegetable Chow Mein*

MILLET AND MUSHROOM BAKE

Cooked millet is soft and fluffy, rather like cooked rice. It makes a welcome change in a vegetarian diet.

Preparation time: 25 minutes
Cooking time: 40 minutes

1 TBSP (3 TSP) **MARMITE** YEAST EXTRACT
450 ML (¾ PINT) BOILING WATER
225 G (8 OZ) MILLET
1 LARGE ONION, FINELY SLICED
4 RASHERS LEAN BACK BACON,
CHOPPED (OPTIONAL)
3 STALKS CELERY, CHOPPED
225 G (8 OZ) CUP MUSHROOMS, SLICED
1 TSP FRESHLY GRATED NUTMEG
(OR ½ TSP GROUND)
1 TBSP CHOPPED FRESH MARJORAM
(OR 1 TSP DRIED)
2 CLOVES GARLIC, CRUSHED
VEGETABLE OIL
SALT AND FRESHLY GROUND BLACK PEPPER
75 G (3 OZ) CHEDDAR CHEESE, GRATED
1 TSP **MARMITE** YEAST EXTRACT

Preheat oven to 200°C (400°F/gas mark 6)

1. Dissolve the MARMITE in the water and place in a saucepan with the millet. Bring to the boil, then cover and simmer for 20-25 minutes until the millet is soft and the water is absorbed.

2. Meanwhile, cook the onion, bacon and celery slowly in a large frying pan until just soft, stirring frequently to prevent sticking. Add the mushrooms and cook for a further 2-3 minutes.

3. Season with the nutmeg and marjoram. Stir in the garlic and add the millet. Mix well.

4. Lightly oil a deep, 20cm (8in) flan dish. Season the mixture to taste and press into the dish. Bake for 15 minutes.

5. Mix together the cheese and second quantity of MARMITE, and spoon over the centre of the mixture. Cook for a further 20-25 minutes, until the cheese has browned. Serve immediately with a side salad.

Serves 4

(without meat option)

MACE IS THE DRIED OUTER HUSK OF THE NUTMEG. ACCORDING TO HISTORICAL RECORDS, A POUND OF MACE ON THE EUROPEAN MARKET IN 1284 WAS WORTH THREE SHEEP OR HALF A COW.

VEGETABLE CHOW MEIN

Chow Mein is usually made with chicken or prawns but is just as delicious when prepared with a good mixture of Oriental-style vegetables. It is the 'gravy' that is considered the great delicacy of this dish.

Preparation time: 15 minutes
Cooking time: 6-8 minutes

250 G (9 OZ) THREAD EGG NOODLES
3 TBSP SESAME OIL
1 LARGE ONION, SLICED
225 G (8 OZ) CHINESE LEAVES, SHREDDED
225 G (8 OZ) CUP MUSHROOMS, SLICED
3 CARROTS, CUT INTO MATCHSTICKS
1 GREEN PEPPER,
DE-SEEDED AND CUT INTO STRIPS
2 CLOVES GARLIC, CRUSHED
GOOD PINCH 5-SPICE POWDER
225 G (8 OZ) BEANSPROUTS
4 TBSP SWEET SHERRY
3 TBSP SOY SAUCE
2 TSP **MARMITE** YEAST EXTRACT
150 ML (¼ PINT) HOT WATER

1. Place the noodles in a large dish, pour boiling water to cover and leave for 4-5 minutes, stirring occasionally.

2. Heat the oil in a wok or large frying pan. Add the onion, Chinese leaves, mushrooms, carrots, pepper and garlic with the 5-spice powder, and stir-fry for 2-3 minutes. Add the beansprouts.

3. Stir the sherry, soy sauce, MARMITE and water into the pan. Drain the noodles and toss them into the vegetables, making certain they are well coated in the sauce.

4. Heat for a couple of minutes, then serve immediately.

Serves 4

IF MAKING A SAUCE IN ADVANCE, LET IT COOL COMPLETELY AND THEN REHEAT GENTLY IN A DOUBLE SAUCEPAN. TO STOP A SKIN FORMING, DOT THE SURFACE OF THE HOT SAUCE WITH TINY PIECES OF BUTTER. THESE WILL MELT AND KEEP THE SURFACE MOIST. ALTERNATIVELY, COVER THE SAUCE WITH BUTTERED GREASEPROOF PAPER.

MICROWAVE

GREEN LENTIL AND MUSHROOM BAKE

This filling supper dish is quick to prepare. Serve with vegetables in season or a colourful mixed salad. If you are a meat-eater, it is delicious with sausages.

Preparation time: 10 minutes
(plus 4 hours or overnight soaking for lentils)
Cooking time: 20 minutes

225G (8OZ) GREEN LENTILS, SOAKED AND DRAINED
1 LARGE ONION, SLICED
125G (4OZ) DRIED APRICOTS, CHOPPED
2 BAY LEAVES
1 TSP MARMITE YEAST EXTRACT
450ML (¾ PINT) BOILING WATER
225G (8OZ) CUP MUSHROOMS, THICKLY SLICED
150ML (¼ PINT) GREEK-STYLE YOGURT
2 TBSP CHOPPED FRESH PARSLEY
SALT AND FRESHLY GROUND BLACK PEPPER
PARSLEY TO GARNISH

Microwave power settings: 100%/Full & 50%

1. Place the lentils, onion, apricots and bay leaves in a large microwave casserole dish. Dissolve the MARMITE in the boiling water and pour into the casserole. Cover and cook for 10 minutes on 100%/Full power.

2. Stir the lentils, add the mushrooms, cover and cook for a further 10 minutes on 50% power.

3. Add the yogurt to the lentils with the parsley, and season to taste. Garnish with a little extra parsley, and serve.

Serves 3-4

VEGETABLE TACOS

Tacos are traditionally filled with a hot beef sauce, topped with salad. This variation is filled with spicy mixed vegetables.

Preparation time: 10 minutes
Cooking time: 20 minutes

675G (1½LB) PREPARED MIXED VEGETABLES
(EG ONIONS, LEEKS, CARROTS, TURNIPS)
1 TSP HOT PEPPER SAUCE
1 TBSP CHILLI SAUCE
1 TSP MARMITE YEAST EXTRACT
500G (1LB 2OZ) PASSATA OR
400G (14OZ) CAN CHOPPED TOMATOES
12 TACO SHELLS
MIXED SALAD ITEMS (INC AVOCADO AND OLIVES),
FINELY SHREDDED OR CHOPPED
GRATED CHEESE

Microwave power setting: 100%/Full

1. Chop or slice all the vegetables and place them in a large microwave dish. Add the sauces, MARMITE and passata. Cover and cook for 10 minutes on 100%/Full power, stirring once. Remove the lid and cook for a further 5 minutes.

2. Remove from the oven, cover, and leave to stand for a few minutes. Place the taco shells on their open side on the turntable and heat for 3 minutes.

3. Spoon a little of the vegetable mixture into each shell, top with the salad and grated cheese. Eat the tacos with your fingers - and have plenty of napkins to hand!

Serves 4

BAKED AUBERGINE DIP

*This has the Mediterranean flavour of pure sunshine!
Use it as a dip or serve it with salad.*

Preparation time: 15 minutes
(plus 30 minutes to salt aubergines)
Cooking time: 10 minutes
Chilling time: 2 hours

2 LARGE AUBERGINES, SLICED

SALT

1 LARGE ONION, CHOPPED

2 CLOVES GARLIC, CRUSHED

4 TBSP OLIVE OIL

1 TBSP TOMATO PURÉE

2 TSP MARMITE YEAST EXTRACT

200G (7OZ) CREAM CHEESE

1 TBSP CHOPPED FRESH OREGANO OR PARSLEY
(OR 1 TSP DRIED)

FRESHLY GROUND BLACK PEPPER

PAPRIKA TO GARNISH

Microwave power setting: 100%/Full

1. Layer the aubergine in a sieve, generously sprinkling each layer with salt. Leave for at least 30 minutes before rinsing thoroughly.

2. Place the aubergine in a suitable microwave dish with the onion, garlic and olive oil. Cover and cook for 10 minutes on 100%/Full power, stirring once.

3. Blend the vegetables with the tomato purée in a liquidiser or food processor, until smooth.

4. Beat the MARMITE into the cream cheese, then add the aubergine purée. Mix well, adding the herbs, and season with pepper to taste.

5. Pile the dip into a serving dish and chill for 2 hours. Garnish with paprika before serving.

Serves 6-8 as a dip, 4 as a salad

TOFU AND SWEET POTATO CURRY

Tofu is a versatile source of protein for vegetarians and is made from bean curd. It does not have much flavour, so I like to spice it up with other ingredients. It is particularly good in curries.

Preparation time: 10 minutes
Cooking time: 20-25 minutes

1 TBSP VEGETABLE OIL

2 TBSP CURRY PASTE

1 TSP MARMITE YEAST EXTRACT

1 LARGE ONION, FINELY SLICED

2 CLOVES GARLIC, CRUSHED

450G (1LB) SWEET POTATO, PEELED AND DICED

400G (14OZ) CAN CHOPPED TOMATOES

285G (10OZ) PACKET TOFU, RINSED,
DRAINED AND DICED

SALT AND FRESHLY GROUND BLACK PEPPER

CHOPPED FRESH CORIANDER
OR PARSLEY TO GARNISH

Microwave power setting: 100%/Full

1. Mix together the oil, curry paste, MARMITE, onion and garlic in a suitable microwave casserole dish. Cover and cook for 3 minutes on 100%/Full power, stirring once.

2. Add the sweet potato and cook for 6 minutes, covered, stirring once; then add the tomatoes and tofu.

3. Cook the curry for a further 10-15 minutes on 100%/Full power, or until the sweet potato is tender. Stir once during cooking.

4. Season to taste, then garnish with coriander or parsley before serving with boiled rice.

Serves 4

If you are following a low-fat diet, you can omit the oil from this recipe.

WASHING LONG-GRAIN RICE IN SEVERAL CHANGES OF WATER
OR IN A SIEVE UNDER RUNNING WATER WILL REMOVE THE
'FLOUR' PRODUCED BY MILLING, WHICH IS WHAT MAKES RICE
STICK TOGETHER IN THE PAN WHEN COOKING.

A GOOD CURRY POWDER SHOULD CONTAIN A COMBINATION OF
MOST OF THE FOLLOWING: PIMENTO, CASSIA, CORIANDER,
CUMIN, FENNEL, GINGER, BLACK AND WHITE PEPPER,
TURMERIC, CAYENNE, CARDAMOM, CLOVES, DILL SEED,
FENUGREEK, NUTMEG AND SALT.

TOP Tofu and Sweet Potato Curry   BOTTOM Turkey Stir-Fry

TOP *Vegetable Tacos*   *BOTTOM* *Baked Aubergine Dip*

TURKEY STIR-FRY

The microwave is marvellous for stir-fry dishes - no smells around the home for ages afterwards! Sesame oil gives a great background flavour to this dish.

Preparation time: 15 minutes
Cooking time: 12-15 minutes

2 TBSP OIL, SESAME OR VEGETABLE
450G (1LB) TURKEY BREAST FILLET,
CUT INTO THIN STRIPS
2 TBSP WHOLEWHEAT FLOUR
1 TSP 5-SPICE POWDER
1 TSP MARMITE YEAST EXTRACT
1 MEDIUM LEEK, FINELY SLICED
2 MEDIUM COURGETTES, CUT INTO MATCHSTICKS
1 SMALL RED PEPPER,
DE-SEEDED AND CUT INTO STRIPS
2 TBSP OYSTER SAUCE

Microwave power setting: 100%/Full

1. Heat the oil in a microwave casserole dish for 2 minutes on 100%/Full power. Toss the turkey in the flour and 5-spice powder, add to the oil and mix well. Cover and cook for 6 minutes, stirring once.

2. Stir in the MARMITE, then add the prepared vegetables and mix well. Cook, uncovered, for 4 minutes, stirring once. Stir in the oyster sauce and serve immediately.

Serves 4

Serve on a bed of egg noodles or rice.

The oil helps to coat the meat with the flour and 5-spice powder, but cut it to 1 tbsp if you are following a low-fat diet.

25G (1OZ) OF COOKED RICE CONTAINS ONLY ABOUT 35 CALORIES, WHICH IS HALF THE CALORIES IN THE SAME WEIGHT OF BREAD.

WHETHER GREEN, RED, YELLOW OR ORANGE, PEPPERS SHOULD HAVE A FIRM, UNWRINKLED SKIN. THEY WILL KEEP FOR A WEEK IN THE SALAD DRAWER OF THE FRIDGE. CUT PEPPERS SHOULD BE CLOSELY COVERED WITH CLING FILM OR KITCHEN FOIL.

SPICED STUFFED PEPPERS

Preparation time: 15 minutes
Cooking time: 30 minutes
Standing time: 5 minutes

4 LARGE GREEN PEPPERS
2 ONIONS, CHOPPED
3 STICKS CELERY, CHOPPED
1/2 TSP GROUND TURMERIC
1 TSP GROUND CUMIN
5CM (2IN) PIECE FRESH GINGER,
PEELED AND GRATED
125G (4OZ) CUP MUSHROOMS, CHOPPED
350G (12OZ) COLD COOKED RICE
50G (2OZ) SULTANAS
50G (2OZ) PISTACHIO KERNELS
OR SALTED PEANUTS
1 TBSP CHOPPED FRESH PARSLEY OR CORIANDER
SALT AND FRESHLY GROUND BLACK PEPPER
1 TSP MARMITE YEAST EXTRACT
1 EGG, BEATEN

Microwave power settings: 100%/Full & 70%

1. Cut the tops off the peppers and keep them. Cut out and discard the cores and seeds. Stand the peppers in a suitable microwave casserole dish. Set to one side.

2. Place the onions, celery, spices and ginger in a covered microwave dish and cook for 6 minutes on 100%/Full power, stirring once. Add the mushrooms and rice and cook for a further 5 minutes, stirring once.

3. Add the sultanas, nuts, parsley or coriander, and salt and pepper. Beat the MARMITE into the egg and use to bind the stuffing together.

4. Fill the peppers with the mixture, pressing down firmly with a teaspoon. Place the tops on the peppers and cover the dish.

5. Cook for 20 minutes on 70% power, or until the peppers are soft. Leave to stand for 5 minutes, then serve with coleslaw or salad.

Serves 4
Ⓥ

TURMERIC IS A BRIGHT YELLOW SPICE USED IN INDIAN COOKING. TAKE CARE WHEN USING IT BECAUSE IT WILL STAIN KITCHEN SURFACES AND TABLE LINEN.

BUCKWHEAT BAKE

This is a variation on the traditional Russian peasant dish, kasha - simple and very tasty.

Preparation time: 10 minutes
Cooking time : 15 minutes
Standing time: 2-3 minutes

1 EGG, BEATEN
450G (1LB) UNROASTED BUCKWHEAT GROATS
2TSP MARMITE YEAST EXTRACT
575ML (1 PINT) BOILING WATER
1 ONION, SLICED
2 LARGE CARROTS, CUT INTO MATCHSTICKS
225G (8OZ) CUP MUSHROOMS, THICKLY SLICED
SALT AND FRESHLY GROUND BLACK PEPPER
1TBSP CHOPPED FRESH PARSLEY

Microwave power settings: 100%/Full & 50%

1. Beat the egg in a suitable microwave casserole dish, add the buckwheat and mix well. Cook, uncovered, on 100%/Full power for 2 minutes, then stir with a fork to separate the groats.

2. Dissolve the MARMITE in the boiling water and add to the dish. Cover and cook for 5 minutes on 100%/Full power.

3. Stir in the prepared vegetables. Cover and cook for a further 6-8 minutes on 50% power, stirring once.

4. Season to taste, and stir in the parsley. Stand for 2-3 minutes before serving.

**Serves 4 as a main course,
6 as an accompaniment**

Buckwheat groats are available in delicatessens and health food shops. When cooked, it is like nutty rice.

CULTIVATED MUSHROOMS ARE GROWN ON STERILISED COMPOST IN A COOL DARK ATMOSPHERE. PEELING THEM IS WASTEFUL, ALL THE GOODNESS IS UNDER THE SKIN. JUST WIPE THEM AND TRIM AWAY STALK-ENDS IF NECESSARY.

BLEND **MARMITE** YEAST EXTRACT WITH BREADCRUMBS TO ADD A SAVOURY FLAVOUR TO COATINGS AND TOPPINGS.

MUSSELS WITH BACON AND MUSHROOMS

Preparation time: 10 minutes
(20 minutes if using live mussels)
Cooking time: 12-15 minutes

900G (2LB) LIVE MUSSELS
OR
450G (1LB) FROZEN COOKED MUSSELS
(WITHOUT SHELLS)
2TBSP OLIVE OIL
1 MEDIUM ONION, FINELY CHOPPED
1 CLOVE GARLIC, CRUSHED
4 RASHERS SMOKED STREAKY BACON, CHOPPED
1TSP MARMITE YEAST EXTRACT
2TBSP TOMATO PURÉE
150ML (¼ PINT) BOILING WATER
1TBSP CHOPPED FRESH PARSLEY
125G (4OZ) CHESTNUT MUSHROOMS, SLICED
SALT AND FRESHLY GROUND BLACK PEPPER
75G (3OZ) EMMENTHAL CHEESE, GRATED

Microwave power setting: 100%/Full

1. Clean the live mussels thoroughly in cold water, removing any barnacles and pulling off the beards. Discard any that have cracked or broken shells.

2. Mix together the oil, onion, garlic and bacon in a large covered microwave dish. Cook, covered, for 4 minutes on 100%/Full power, stirring once.

3. Mix together the MARMITE, tomato purée and water and add to the dish with the parsley and mushrooms. Add a little salt and pepper and the mussels. Mix together carefully, then cover and cook for 5-6 minutes, stirring once. (Live mussels should be cooked until all the shells have opened fully, so add an extra minute or so to the cooking time if necessary.)

4. Scatter the cheese over the mussels and cook for a further 1-2 minutes, until the cheese is melted. Serve immediately.

Serves 3-4

You may prefer to remove half the shell when using fresh mussels, after they have cooked and before adding the cheese – it looks neater!

The mussels may be arranged on individual serving dishes and the cheese browned under a pre-heated grill, if preferred.

A D U K I   A N D   D A T E
C A S S E R O L E

Preparation time: 15 minutes
(plus overnight soaking for beans)
Cooking time: 40 minutes

1 LARGE ONION, CHOPPED
1 BULB FENNEL, TRIMMED AND CHOPPED
1 RED PEPPER, DE-SEEDED AND SLICED
2 COURGETTES, TRIMMED AND SLICED
225G (8OZ) ADUKI BEANS, SOAKED AND DRAINED
2 TSP MARMITE YEAST EXTRACT
450ML (³/₄ PINT) BOILING WATER
1 TBSP DEMERARA SUGAR (OR TO TASTE)
1 TBSP TOMATO PURÉE
125G (4OZ) CHOPPED PITTED DATES
SALT AND FRESHLY GROUND BLACK PEPPER
1 TBSP CHOPPED FRESH CORIANDER OR PARSLEY
ZEST OF ORANGE TO GARNISH

Microwave power settings: 100%/Full & 50%

1. Cook the onion and fennel together in a large covered microwave dish for 4-5 minutes on 100%/Full power, stirring once.

2. Add the pepper, courgettes and beans. Dissolve the MARMITE in the boiling water and mix with the sugar and tomato purée. Pour into the dish. Add the chopped dates.

3. Cover and cook for 10 minutes on 100%/Full power; then stir, cover and cook for a further 20-30 minutes on 50% power, until the sauce is thickened and the beans are cooked.

4. Season to taste. Mix together the coriander or parsley and orange zest and scatter over the dish just before serving.

Serves 4-6

S P I C E D   L A M B   W I T H
A U B E R G I N E

Lamb and aubergine is a perfect combination of flavours and is further enhanced with tomatoes and Mozzarella cheese.

Preparation time: 10 minutes
Cooking time: 30 minutes

1 AUBERGINE, SLICED
1 LARGE ONION, FINELY SLICED
2 TBSP OLIVE OIL
2 RASHERS BACK BACON, CHOPPED
450G (1LB) MINCED LAMB
1 TSP MARMITE YEAST EXTRACT
1 TBSP CHOPPED FRESH MIXED HERBS
(OR 1 TSP DRIED)
400G (14OZ) CAN CHOPPED TOMATOES
FRESHLY GROUND BLACK PEPPER
125G (4OZ) MOZZARELLA CHEESE, GRATED

Microwave power settings: 100%/Full & 50%

1. Place the aubergine, onion and olive oil in a covered microwave casserole and cook for 6 minutes on 100%/Full power, stirring once. Using a slotted spoon, remove the vegetables from the casserole.

2. Place the bacon in the casserole with the minced lamb. Cover and cook for 4 minutes on 100%/Full power, stirring once.

3. Stir in the MARMITE, add the herbs and the chopped tomatoes and cook for a further 10 minutes, covered, stirring once during cooking. Season to taste with black pepper.

4. Place the aubergines and onions in a layer on top of the lamb, then top with the cheese.

5. Cook, uncovered, for a further 10 minutes on 50% power. Serve immediately.

Serves 4

DEEP-FRIED PARSLEY MAKES AN ATTRACTIVE AND UNUSUAL GARNISH. HOLD A SPRIG OF PARSLEY BY A LENGTH OF KITCHEN STRING AND LOWER IT INTO HOT DEEP OIL. IN A FEW SECONDS THE PARSLEY WILL BE CRISP AND A BRILLIANT GREEN.

TWO TEASPOONS OF **MARMITE** YEAST EXTRACT TO ONE PINT OF WATER MAKES A GOOD STOCK FOR ANY SAVOURY DISH.

REDUCE YOUR FAT INTAKE BY SKIMMING FAT OFF GRAVY, CASSEROLES OR SAUCES. ONE WAY IS TO LAY SHEETS OF ABSORBENT KITCHEN PAPER ON THE SURFACE, LIFT AND DISCARD.

TOP Aduki and Date Casserole   *CENTRE* Spiced Lamb with Aubergine   *BOTTOM* Mussels with Bacon and Mushrooms

PIZZAS & PASTAS

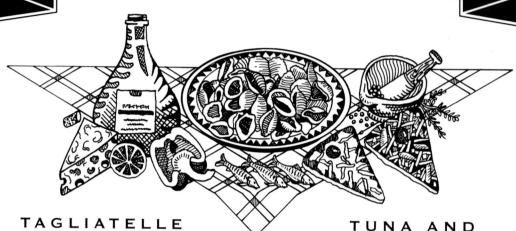

TAGLIATELLE TUSCANY-STYLE

Preparation time: 10 minutes
Cooking time: 10 minutes

SALT
VEGETABLE OIL
225G (8OZ) TAGLIATELLE
50G (2OZ) BUTTER OR MARGARINE
2TSP MARMITE YEAST EXTRACT
450G (1LB) COURGETTES, SLICED
225G (8OZ) CUP MUSHROOMS, SLICED
SALT AND FRESHLY GROUND BLACK PEPPER
50G (2OZ) PARMESAN CHEESE, GRATED

1. Bring a large pan of water, with a little salt and oil, to the boil. Cook the tagliatelle as directed on the packet and drain.

2. While the pasta is cooking, melt the butter in a large pan and add the MARMITE. Cook the courgettes in the butter for 4-5 minutes, then add the mushrooms and cook for a further 2-3 minutes. Season to taste.

3. Add the drained pasta and the cheese, and mix well. Serve with a green salad and garlic bread.

Serves 3-4

If you use butter to cook the courgettes, do so on a low heat or else the butter will turn black. A drop of olive oil added to the pan will prevent this happening.

TUNA AND HORSERADISH PASTA

If you think you've tried every possible pasta and tuna combination, don't pass this one by. It surprised even my tastebuds!

Preparation time: 15 minutes
Cooking time: 10 minutes

SALT
VEGETABLE OIL
350G (12OZ) PASTA SHAPES
350G (12OZ) CAULIFLOWER FLORETS
25G (1OZ) BUTTER
125G (4OZ) CUP MUSHROOMS, SLICED
200ML (7FL OZ) SINGLE OR WHIPPING CREAM
200G (7OZ) CAN TUNA IN BRINE, DRAINED
1TSP HORSERADISH SAUCE
1TSP MARMITE YEAST EXTRACT
SALT AND FRESHLY GROUND BLACK PEPPER
1TBSP CHOPPED FRESH PARSLEY
(OR 1TSP DRIED)

1. Bring a large pan of water, with a little salt and oil, to the boil. Cook the pasta and cauliflower together in the water for 10 minutes, or as directed on the packet. Drain and keep warm.

2. Melt the butter in a large pan and add the mushrooms. Cook for 2-3 minutes. Add the cream, bring to the boil and cook quickly for 2-3 minutes, until slightly reduced and thickened.

3. Add the tuna, horseradish and MARMITE, then mix with the pasta and cauliflower. Stir over a low heat to warm through. Season to taste and garnish with parsley. Serve with a tomato and basil salad.

Serves 4

SARDINIAN PIZZA

Sardine and blue cheese is one of my favourite combinations of flavours, whether it be for a quiche or a pizza. It is an unusual pizza topping as it relies on the sauce from the sardines for the tomato flavour.

Preparation time: 15 minutes
Cooking time: 10 minutes

2 READY-PREPARED 25CM (10IN) PIZZA BASES
2 TBSP OLIVE OIL
1 LARGE ONION, FINELY CHOPPED
1 RED PEPPER, DE-SEEDED AND CHOPPED
125G (4OZ) CUP MUSHROOMS, SLICED
1 TSP MARMITE YEAST EXTRACT
FRESHLY GROUND BLACK PEPPER
2 x 120G (4OZ) CANS SARDINES IN TOMATO SAUCE
125G (4OZ) GORGONZOLA
(OR ANY BLUE CHEESE), CRUMBLED
1 TBSP CHOPPED FRESH PARSLEY
(OR 1 TSP DRIED)

Preheat oven to 220°C (425°F/gas mark 7)

1. Place the pizza bases on two lightly greased baking sheets.

2. Heat the oil in a frying pan, add the onion and pepper and cook until soft. Add the mushrooms and cook for a further 4-5 minutes. Stir the MARMITE into the vegetables and season to taste, then spread the mixture over the pizza bases.

3. Arrange one can of sardines on each pizza, pouring the tomato sauce over the topping. Scatter the cheese on top and garnish with parsley.

4. Bake in the oven for 10 minutes, and serve immediately.

Makes 2

SEAFOOD PASTA

This can be prepared at short notice, almost from the store cupboard.

Preparation time: 15 minutes
Cooking time: 30 minutes

185G (6½OZ) CAN TUNA IN OIL
1 ONION, FINELY CHOPPED
SALT
VEGETABLE OIL
400G (14OZ) CAN CHOPPED TOMATOES
1 TBSP CHOPPED FRESH PARSLEY
(OR 1 TSP DRIED)
1 TSP MARMITE YEAST EXTRACT
225G (8OZ) PASTA SHELLS OR TWIRLS
170G (6OZ) CAN CRAB MEAT, DRAINED
142G (5OZ) JAR COCKLES OR MUSSELS,
DRAINED AND RINSED
150ML (5FL OZ) SOURED CREAM
OR THICK NATURAL YOGURT
SALT AND FRESHLY GROUND BLACK PEPPER
CHOPPED FRESH PARSLEY FOR GARNISH

1. Drain the oil from the tuna into a saucepan, add the onion and cook slowly for 3-4 minutes, until soft. Meanwhile bring a large pan of water, with a little salt and oil, to the boil.

2. Add the tomatoes, parsley and MARMITE to the onion and simmer for 10-15 minutes, until slightly reduced and thickened.

3. When the water boils, add the pasta and cook for 10 minutes, or as directed on the packet. Drain and rinse with boiling water.

4. Add the tuna, crab, and cockles or mussels to the tomato sauce. Heat through for 3-4 minutes, then stir in the soured cream or yogurt and continue to heat gently for a further 2-3 minutes. Season to taste.

5. Mix the sauce into the pasta and heat through. Garnish with extra parsley and serve immediately.

Serves 4

IF YOU HAVE PROBLEMS CUTTING UP COOKED PIZZAS - TRY USING THE KITCHEN SCISSORS!

ADD **MARMITE** YEAST EXTRACT TO CHEESE SAUCE TO REDUCE THE AMOUNT OF CHEESE NEEDED TO GIVE A GOOD STRONG FLAVOUR.

PASTA PERFECTION IS REACHED WHEN IT IS COOKED **AL DENTE**. THIS LITERALLY MEANS 'TO THE TOOTH', IE WHEN IT STILL HAS SOME BITE TO IT AND IS NOT SOGGY AND OVERCOOKED.

TOP Four Cheeses Pizza   CENTRE Seafood Pasta   BOTTOM Pizza Firenze

PIZZA FIRENZE

If you like hot and spicy food, this is the perfect pizza for you!

Preparation time: 20 minutes
Cooking time: 10 minutes

2 READY-PREPARED 25CM (10IN) PIZZA BASES
1 LARGE ONION, FINELY CHOPPED
1 CLOVE GARLIC, CRUSHED
1 GREEN CHILLI,
DE-SEEDED AND VERY FINELY CHOPPED
1 TBSP OLIVE OIL
400G (14OZ) CAN CHOPPED TOMATOES
1 TBSP HOT PEPPER SAUCE (OR TO TASTE)
1 TSP MARMITE YEAST EXTRACT
FRESHLY GROUND BLACK PEPPER
150G (5OZ) KABANOS,
OR OTHER SPICY SAUSAGE, SLICED
50G (2OZ) CAN ANCHOVY FILLETS
75G (3OZ) MOZZARELLA CHEESE, GRATED
CAPERS OR GHERKINS TO GARNISH

Preheat oven to 220°C (425°F/gas mark 7)

1. Place the pizza bases on two lightly greased baking sheets.

2. Cook the onion, garlic and chilli in the oil for 3-4 minutes, until soft. Add the tomatoes, pepper sauce and MARMITE, and simmer for 10 minutes until reduced and thickened. Season to taste with pepper, then spread the sauce over the pizza bases.

3. Scatter the sausage slices over the pizzas and arrange the anchovy fillets on top. Top with the cheese and garnish with capers or gherkins.

4. Bake in the oven for 10 minutes and serve immediately.

Makes 2

If you like the flavour of anchovies, brush the pizza bases with the oil from the fish fillets before adding the tomato sauce.

FOUR CHEESES PIZZA

Usually the four cheeses are kept separate on this pizza. But you get a better flavour if you mix them up.

Preparation time: 20 minutes
Cooking time: 10 minutes

2 READY-PREPARED 25CM (10IN) PIZZA BASES
1 LARGE ONION, FINELY CHOPPED
1 PEPPER, DE-SEEDED AND DICED
2 TBSP OLIVE OIL
400G (14OZ) CAN CHOPPED TOMATOES
1 CLOVE GARLIC, CRUSHED
1 TSP MARMITE YEAST EXTRACT
1 TBSP CHOPPED FRESH MARJORAM OR OREGANO
(OR 1 TSP DRIED)
SALT AND FRESHLY GROUND BLACK PEPPER
75G (3OZ) CHEDDAR CHEESE, GRATED
75G (3OZ) DOLCELATTE (OR ANY BLUE CHEESE),
CRUMBLED
50G (2OZ) PARMESAN CHEESE, GRATED
75G (3OZ) MOZZARELLA CHEESE, GRATED
OLIVES FOR GARNISH

Preheat oven to 220°C (425°F/gas mark 7)

1. Place the pizza bases on two lightly greased baking sheets.

2. Cook the onion and pepper in the oil until soft. Add the tomatoes, garlic, MARMITE, herbs and seasonings. Simmer for 10-15 minutes.

3. Spoon the sauce onto the pizza bases, then top with the four cheeses, finishing with the Mozzarella. Garnish with olives.

4. Bake in the oven for 10 minutes, until the cheese is melted and the bases are browned. Serve immediately.

Makes 2

MOZZARELLA IS A SOFT ITALIAN CHEESE ORIGINALLY MADE FROM BUFFALO MILK, BUT NOW USUALLY MADE FROM COWS' MILK. TRADITIONALLY IT WAS MADE IN SMALL BALLS AND KEPT DANGLING FROM STRING IN VATS OF WEAK BRINE.

PIZZA PLUS

Preparation time: 20 minutes
Cooking time: 10 minutes

2 READY-PREPARED 25CM (10IN) PIZZA BASES
1 ONION, CHOPPED
2 TBSP OLIVE OIL
400G (14OZ) CAN CHOPPED TOMATOES
1 TBSP TOMATO PURÉE
1 TSP MARMITE YEAST EXTRACT
75G (3OZ) CHEDDAR
OR MOZZARELLA CHEESE, GRATED
1 TBSP CHOPPED FRESH PARSLEY
(OR 1 TSP DRIED)

PLUS YOUR CHOICE OF:
400G (14OZ) CAN ARTICHOKE HEARTS,
DRAINED AND HALVED
175G (6OZ) CUP MUSHROOMS, SLICED
1 PEPPER, DE-SEEDED AND CHOPPED
125G (4OZ) SWEETCORN
1 MEDIUM CARROT, FINELY DICED

Preheat oven to 220°C (425°F/gas mark 7)

1. Place the pizza bases on two lightly greased baking sheets.

2. Cook the onion in the oil until soft, then add the tomatoes, purée and MARMITE. Add your choice of extra ingredients and simmer for 10-15 minutes, until slightly thickened.

3. Spread the sauce over the pizza bases, then divide the cheese between the two. Scatter a little parsley over each pizza.

4. Bake in the oven for 10 minutes. Serve immediately.

Makes 2

If you are in a hurry or don't have a big appetite you can always settle for the basic cheese and tomato pizza, minus the pluses.

SPAGHETTI SUPREMO

Bolognese sauce has so many variations that it has almost come to mean any meat sauce that you serve with pasta. This recipe uses a variety of meats to achieve a good rich flavour with only nutmeg as additional seasoning.

Preparation time: 15 minutes
Cooking time: 1-1½ hours

1 LARGE ONION, FINELY CHOPPED
1 TBSP OLIVE OIL
225G (8OZ) MINCED BEEF
225G (8OZ) MINCED PORK
225G (8OZ) CHICKEN LIVERS, CHOPPED
150ML (¼ PINT) RED WINE
2 TBSP TOMATO PURÉE
2 TSP MARMITE YEAST EXTRACT
1 TSP GROUND NUTMEG
SALT AND FRESHLY GROUND BLACK PEPPER
225G (8OZ) SPAGHETTI
PARMESAN CHEESE, GRATED, FOR SERVING

1. Cook the onion in the oil in a large saucepan, until soft. Add the beef and pork and cook for 3-4 minutes over a high heat, until browned. Add the chicken livers and cook for a further 2-3 minutes, until also browned.

2. Add the wine and cook rapidly for a few minutes, until reduced, then add the tomato purée, MARMITE, nutmeg, salt and pepper. Stir well, cover the pan and simmer slowly for at least 1 hour - the longer and slower the cooking, the better the flavour.

3. Bring a large pan of water to the boil, with a little salt and oil. Cook the spaghetti for about 10 minutes, or as directed on the packet. Drain thoroughly and rinse with boiling water.

4. Season the sauce to taste, then serve with the spaghetti, topped with Parmesan cheese.

Serves 4

The Italians always mix their sauces into the cooked pasta, rather than serving the sauce on a pasta nest.

IF YOU ARE PRONE TO WEEPING WHEN PEELING ONIONS, TRY COOKING WITH SPANISH VARIETIES. THEY ARE MILDER THAN ENGLISH OR EGYPTIAN ONIONS.

WHEN A RECIPE CALLS FOR 'A GLASS OF WINE' IT USUALLY MEANS APPROXIMATELY 75-100ML (3-4FL OZ), NOT A LARGE DRINKING GLASS.

LENTIL AND AUBERGINE LASAGNE

Preparation time: 30 minutes
Cooking time: 30-40 minutes

LENTIL SAUCE:

1 LARGE ONION, SLICED
1 RED PEPPER, DE-SEEDED AND DICED
2 TBSP OLIVE OIL
1 AUBERGINE, HALVED AND SLICED
125G (4OZ) RED LENTILS
400G (14OZ) CAN CHOPPED TOMATOES
1 TBSP (3 TSP) MARMITE YEAST EXTRACT
300ML (½ PINT) BOILING WATER
1 TBSP CHOPPED FRESH OREGANO
(OR 1 TSP DRIED)
2 BAY LEAVES
SALT AND FRESHLY GROUND BLACK PEPPER

CHEESE SAUCE:

50G (2OZ) BUTTER OR MARGARINE
50G (2OZ) FLOUR
575ML (1 PINT) MILK
125G (4OZ) CHEDDAR CHEESE, GRATED
PINCH NUTMEG
SALT AND FRESHLY GROUND BLACK PEPPER

8 SHEETS NO-COOK LASAGNE

Preheat oven to 200°C (400°F/gas mark 6)

1. To prepare the lentil sauce, cook the onion and pepper in the oil for 2-3 minutes until soft, then add the aubergine and cook for a further 3-4 minutes, stirring regularly. Add the lentils and tomatoes. Dissolve the MARMITE in the boiling water and add to the pan with the seasonings. Cover and simmer for 20 minutes.

2. To prepare the cheese sauce, melt the butter or margarine in a pan, add the flour to make a roux and cook slowly for 30 seconds. Remove from the heat and gradually add the milk. Bring the sauce slowly to the boil, stirring constantly until it thickens. Add a little of the cheese with some nutmeg, and season to taste.

3. Place a layer of the lentil sauce in the base of an ovenproof dish. Cover with half the pasta, in a single layer, then repeat with the remaining sauce and lasagne. Top with the cheese sauce and sprinkle on the remaining cheese.

4. Bake for 30-40 minutes, until browned.

Serves 4

If you need to add a little more liquid to the lentil sauce, mix 1 tsp MARMITE with 150ml (¼ pint) boiling water. The sauce should be fairly runny as the lasagne will absorb some of the liquid. The sauce can also be used with spaghetti.

PIZZA CALZONE

This is a folded pizza that looks like a Cornish pasty! You make your own dough and can fill it with almost anything you like.

Preparation time: 30 minutes
Proving time: 30 minutes
Cooking time: 15 minutes

PIZZA BASE:

450G (1 LB) STRONG WHITE FLOUR
7G (¼OZ) SACHET FAST-ACTING YEAST
150ML (¼ PINT) OLIVE OIL
1 TBSP (3 TSP) MARMITE YEAST EXTRACT
300ML (½ PINT) WARM WATER (APPROX)

FILLING:

1 LARGE ONION, CHOPPED
1 CLOVE GARLIC, CRUSHED
1 PEPPER, DE-SEEDED AND FINELY CHOPPED
1 TBSP OLIVE OIL
125G (4OZ) CUP MUSHROOMS, SLICED
6 TOMATOES, SLICED
175G (6OZ) SLICED HAM OR SALAMI, CHOPPED
125G (4OZ) CHEDDAR OR MOZZARELLA CHEESE,
GRATED
1 TBSP CHOPPED FRESH OREGANO
(OR 1 TSP DRIED)

Preheat oven to 220°C (425°F/gas mark 7)

1. Place the flour in a large bowl and mix in the yeast. Make a well in the centre and add the oil. Dissolve the MARMITE in the warm water and add to the bowl gradually, to make a pliable, manageable dough.

2. Knead thoroughly on a floured surface until smooth, and divide into four equal pieces. Shape each piece into a circle about 20cm (8in) in diameter. Place on two lightly oiled baking sheets, cover and leave to rise in a warm place for 30 minutes.

3. To prepare the filling: cook the onion, garlic and pepper in the olive oil until soft. Pile the mixture onto the risen pizza bases, top with the mushrooms, tomatoes, ham or salami and scatter the cheese over. Sprinkle with oregano.

4. Dampen the edges of the dough and fold the pizzas over, sealing and crimping the edges. Place on the prepared baking sheets and bake for 15 minutes. Serve immediately.

Makes 4

When proving dough, put it on a lightly oiled baking sheet and place inside a lightly oiled plastic bag. Seal and leave in a warm place to rise.

Top Pizza Calzone   Left Tagliatelle Marmesto

RIGHT Coronation Pasta   BOTTOM Lentil and Aubergine Lasagne

CORONATION PASTA

Coronation Chicken and Pasta Salad are two popular dishes. This recipe combines the best of both, in one delicious salad.

Preparation time: 15 minutes
(plus 45 minutes to cook and cool the pasta)
Chilling time: 1 hour

350G (12OZ) SMALL PASTA SHELLS
300ML (½ PINT) MAYONNAISE
2 TBSP MANGO CHUTNEY
1 TBSP (3 TSP) MARMITE YEAST EXTRACT
1 RED CHILLI, DE-SEEDED AND FINELY CHOPPED
FRESHLY GROUND BLACK PEPPER
225G (8OZ) COOKED CHICKEN, DICED
225G (8OZ) SEEDLESS GRAPES, HALVED
LOLLO ROSSO LETTUCE OR RAW SPINACH
PAPRIKA
1 TBSP CHOPPED FRESH CORIANDER OR PARSLEY

1. Cook the pasta. Rinse in cold water, drain well and cool.

2. Mix together the mayonnaise, chutney, MARMITE, and the chilli. Season to taste, then stir in the chicken.

3. Add the pasta gradually, stirring well to make certain it is evenly coated in the sauce. Finally, add the grapes and transfer to a salad bowl or platter lined with lollo rosso lettuce leaves or raw spinach.

4. Sprinkle a little paprika over the salad. If fresh coriander or parsley is available, scatter it over the salad as a second garnish.

5. Chill for 1 hour before serving.

Serves 6-8

Coriander is available at most large supermarkets. It is easy to grow in the garden, but too tall for window boxes as it reaches a height of over 1 metre. After flowering, wait for the seeds to form, then collect and dry them. They are delicious crushed in curries, rice dishes or with lamb.

TAGLIATELLE MARMESTO

Pesto is a traditional Italian pasta sauce, made with basil, olive oil, pine nuts and Parmesan cheese - ingredients that are comparatively cheap in Italy. This adaptation of the traditional sauce is well worth making at home in preference to a shop-bought variety.

Preparation time: 15 minutes
Cooking time: 10 minutes

50G (2OZ) FRESH PARSLEY
25G (1OZ) FRESH BASIL
1 TSP MARMITE YEAST EXTRACT
SALT AND FRESHLY GROUND BLACK PEPPER
2 CLOVES GARLIC, CRUSHED
90G (3½OZ) NATURALLY ROASTED PEANUTS
(NOT SALTED)
50G (2OZ) PARMESAN CHEESE, GRATED
(PREFERABLY FRESH)
200ML (7 FL OZ) VIRGIN OLIVE OIL
450G (1 LB) TAGLIATELLE, SPAGHETTI
OR OTHER PASTA

1. Place all the ingredients for the sauce, except the olive oil, in a liquidiser or food processor. Switch on, and gradually add the olive oil, working the mixture to a fairly smooth paste.

2. Bring a large pan of water, with a little salt and oil, to the boil. Cook the pasta for 10 minutes, or as directed. Drain and return to the pan.

3. Over a very low heat stir in the Marmesto sauce, ensuring that all the pasta is well coated. The amount of sauce above will serve 6-8 people, allowing about one heaped tablespoon per person.

4. Serve the pasta immediately; it really needs no accompaniment.

Serves 6-8

SAVOURIES & SNACKS

GINGER AND CORIANDER PINWHEELS

Preparation time: 10 minutes
Chilling time : 2 hours

**8 SLICES FROM MEDIUM SANDWICH LOAF,
CRUSTS REMOVED**
1 TSP MARMITE YEAST EXTRACT
2 TBSP MAYONNAISE
**90G (3½OZ) CRYSTALLISED GINGER,
ROUGHLY CHOPPED**
2 TBSP CHOPPED FRESH CORIANDER

1. Roll the slices of bread lightly with a rolling pin to flatten.

2. Mix the MARMITE with the mayonnaise and spread on the bread.

3. Blend the ginger and coriander together in a liquidiser or food processor to form a smooth paste. Spread this over the bread, then roll up each slice and wrap tightly in individual pieces of foil. Chill for 2 hours.

4. Unwrap the rolls and slice them into 4-6 pieces each.

Serves 6

APPLE RAREBIT

Preparation time: 5 minutes
Cooking time: 8-10 minutes

4 SLICES BREAD
BUTTER OR MAYONNAISE
MARMITE YEAST EXTRACT TO TASTE
**175G (6OZ) WENSLEYDALE
OR LANCASHIRE CHEESE, GRATED**
EATING APPLE, PEELED AND GRATED
½ TSP MUSTARD

1. Toast the bread on one side only. Butter or spread the bread with mayonnaise, then spread with MARMITE.

2. Mix together the cheese, apple and mustard. Pile onto the bread and grill for 3-4 minutes, until the cheese is melted and bubbling. Serve immediately.

Serves 4

MAKE YOUR OWN SPECIAL NUT MIXTURE FOR NIBBLING WITH DRINKS BY FRYING YOUR CHOICE OF NUTS IN A LITTLE OIL OR BUTTER UNTIL GOLDEN. STIR IN GROUND SPICES WHILE FRYING, OR SPRINKLE WITH GROUND SEA SALT WHILE STILL WARM.

USING A KNIFE RINSED WITH VERY HOT WATER MAKES CUTTING CRUMBLY CHEESE EASIER.

PEPPER TARTLETS

Bite-sized quiches made with pastry flavoured with MARMITE, and a pepper and cream cheese filling.

Preparation time: 20 minutes
Cooking time: 25 minutes

PASTRY:
125G (4OZ) PLAIN FLOUR
50G (2OZ) BUTTER OR MARGARINE
2TSP MARMITE YEAST EXTRACT
WATER TO MIX

FILLING:
1/2 SMALL GREEN PEPPER,
DE-SEEDED AND VERY FINELY CHOPPED
1 TBSP OLIVE OIL
1 EGG, BEATEN
50G (2OZ) SOFT CHEESE
WITH GARLIC AND PARSLEY
75ML (3FL OZ) MILK
SALT AND FRESHLY GROUND BLACK PEPPER

Preheat oven to 200°C (400°F/gas mark 6)

1. Lightly grease 12 patty tins (1 tray).

2. Rub the butter or margarine into the flour for the pastry, until the mixture resembles fine breadcrumbs. Stir in the MARMITE and add sufficient water to mix to a firm but manageable dough. Roll out and use to line the patty tins.

3. Cook the pepper in the olive oil until soft (about 3-4 minutes), then divide between the tartlets.

4. Beat the remaining ingredients together in a bowl with a fork and carefully fill the tartlets with the mixture.

5. Place in the oven, reduce the temperature to 180°C (350°F/gas mark 4) and bake for 25 minutes. Cool on a wire rack.

Makes 12

Press the pastry well down into the patty tins, otherwise it may rise up during cooking and you will lose all the filling from the tartlets.

DEVILS ON HORSEBACK

Preparation time: 15 minutes
Cooking time: 10-15 minutes

6 SLICES FROM WHITE SANDWICH LOAF
VEGETABLE OIL
12 RASHERS STREAKY BACON
1 TBSP (3TSP) MARMITE YEAST EXTRACT
(OR TO TASTE)
24 READY-TO-EAT PITTED PRUNES

WOODEN COCKTAIL STICKS

Preheat oven to 200°C (400°F/gas mark 6)

1. Using a shaped cutter, make four large croutons from each slice of bread. Heat some oil in a frying pan and shallow fry the croutons for a few seconds on each side, until lightly browned. Remove from the pan with a slotted spoon and drain on kitchen paper.

2. Stretch the bacon with the back of a knife to make it thinner, then cut each rasher in half. Spread the bacon with a little MARMITE, then roll each half rasher around a prune. Secure it to a crouton with a cocktail stick and place on a baking sheet.

3. Bake in the oven for 10-15 minutes, until the bacon is cooked. Allow to cool slightly before serving as the prunes become very hot.

Makes 24

THE USE OF YEAST IN THE MAKING OF WINE, BEER AND BREAD DATES BACK THOUSANDS OF YEARS, BUT IT WASN'T UNTIL THE LATE 19TH CENTURY THAT A YEAST EXTRACT WAS SUCCESSFULLY DEVELOPED. PIONEERS IN THE FIELD WERE THE FRENCH BACTERIOLOGIST LOUIS PASTEUR AND THE GERMAN CHEMIST JUSTUS VON LIEBIG. **MARMITE** YEAST EXTRACT, CLOSE ON THE HEELS OF THIS SCIENTIFIC BREAKTHROUGH, WAS FIRST MANUFACTURED IN ENGLAND IN 1902.

TRY GRINDING BLACK PEPPER ONTO STRAWBERRIES OR FRESH FIGS AND SERVE WITHOUT CREAM. SOUNDS STRANGE, TASTES DELICIOUSLY DIFFERENT.

TOP LEFT Pepper Tartlets   TOP RIGHT Ginger and Coriander Pinwheels   BOTTOM LEFT Devils on Horseback   BOTTOM RIGHT Apple Rarebit

CHEESE AND HAM COCOTTES

These are quick to assemble and relatively low in fat. There is plenty of time to prepare a side salad for serving while the cocottes are in the oven.

Preparation time: 10 minutes
Cooking time: 30 minutes

VEGETABLE OIL
1 TSP MARMITE YEAST EXTRACT
175G (6OZ) COTTAGE CHEESE, SIEVED
2 EGGS, BEATEN
3 TBSP THICK NATURAL YOGURT
(GREEK-STYLE OR SET)
SALT AND FRESHLY GROUND BLACK PEPPER
175G (6OZ) HAM, CHOPPED
CHOPPED FRESH PARSLEY FOR GARNISH

Preheat oven to 180°C (350°F/gas mark 4)

1. Lightly oil four ramekin dishes and place them in a shallow *bain Marie* (water bath).

2. Beat the MARMITE into the cottage cheese, then add all the remaining ingredients and mix well. Spoon the mixture into the ramekins.

3. Bake in the oven for 30 minutes, or until set. Sprinkle with chopped parsley and serve immediately.

Serves 4

SMOKED MACKEREL PÂTÉ

This is spicier than most fish pâtés.

Preparation time: 10 minutes
Chilling time: 2 hours

450G (1LB) SMOKED MACKEREL FILLETS
200G (7OZ) CREAM CHEESE
2.5CM (1IN) PIECE FRESH GINGER,
PEELED AND GRATED
1 GREEN CHILLI, DE-SEEDED AND CHOPPED
2 TSP MARMITE YEAST EXTRACT
2 TBSP CHOPPED FRESH PARSLEY
SALT AND FRESHLY GROUND BLACK PEPPER

1. Skin the mackerel fillets and break into small pieces. Then place with all the remaining ingredients in a liquidiser or food processor and blend until well mixed and smooth.

2. Season to taste, then pile the pâté into a serving dish and chill for at least 2 hours. Serve with bread, oatcakes or freshly cooked toast.

Serves 4-6

TO CHOP CHIVES OR SPRING ONIONS EASILY AND QUICKLY, HOLD THEM IN A BUNCH IN ONE HAND AND SNIP WITH KITCHEN SCISSORS.

THE MUCH-HERALDED NUTRITIONAL VALUE AND VERSATILITY OF **MARMITE** YEAST EXTRACT ENSURED THAT THE PRODUCT WAS 'CALLED UP' FOR SERVICE IN TWO WORLD WARS, AS WELL AS BEING IN GREAT DEMAND AMONG ALLIED POWS. FOR THE SAME REASON, IT IS AN ALMOST AUTOMATIC CHOICE FOR THINGS LIKE MOUNTAINEERING AND POLAR EXPEDITIONS - WHERE EVERY SPOONFUL COUNTS.

MAKE YOUR OWN MELBA TOAST TO SERVE WITH PÂTÉS AND SOUPS. CUT OFF CRUSTS FROM FRESHLY MADE SLICES OF TOAST AND SPLIT EACH SLICE IN HALF HORIZONTALLY. BAKE THE HALVES IN A HOT OVEN TILL THEY CURL UP SLIGHTLY AND ARE WELL BROWNED AND CRISP.

FLAVOURED VINEGARS ADD A SUBTLE DIFFERENCE TO SALAD DRESSINGS. MAKE HERB VINEGARS BY INFUSING A HANDFUL OF THE FRESH HERB IN WHITE WINE VINEGAR FOR ABOUT TWO WEEKS BEFORE USING. TRY TARRAGON, BASIL OR MARJORAM.

EGGS FLORENTINE ON TOAST

Preparation time: 5 minutes
Cooking time: 10 minutes

675G (1½LB) FROZEN CHOPPED SPINACH
4 EGGS
1TBSP (3TSP) MARMITE YEAST EXTRACT
4 SLICES FRESHLY COOKED TOAST
FRESHLY GROUND BLACK PEPPER

1. Cook the spinach as directed on the packet. Drain in a sieve, squeezing out as much water as possible.

2. Heat some water in a small frying pan or egg poacher and cook the eggs for 3-4 minutes, or to your liking.

3. Beat the MARMITE into the drained spinach, then pile it onto the toast, making a dip in the centre of the spinach.

4. Serve immediately, topping each slice of toast with a poached egg. Season with pepper.

Serves 4

SAVOURY PETITS CHOUX

Preparation time: 35 minutes
Cooking time: 40 minutes
Cooling time: 1 hour

CHOUX PASTRY:
50G (2OZ) BUTTER
150ML (¼ PINT) WATER
65G (2½OZ) STRONG PLAIN FLOUR, SIEVED
2 EGGS, BEATEN

FILLING:
200G (7OZ) CREAM CHEESE
25G (1OZ) BUTTER
1TSP ENGLISH MUSTARD
1TSP HORSERADISH SAUCE
1TSP MARMITE YEAST EXTRACT

GARNISH:
MARMITE YEAST EXTRACT TO TASTE
1TBSP FINELY CHOPPED FRESH PARSLEY

Preheat oven to 220°C (425°F/gas mark 7)

1. Lightly grease a large baking sheet.

2. Place the butter and water in a pan and bring to a rapid boil, making certain the fat has melted. Shoot in the flour, beating vigorously and removing the pan from the heat. Beat until the pastry forms a ball and leaves the sides of the pan. Cool slightly, then gradually beat in the eggs to give a smooth, soft mixture that will hold its shape.

3. Pipe small mounds of pastry onto the baking sheet, or use two teaspoons to form walnut-sized shapes. Bake for 20 minutes.

4. Remove the pastry from the oven and slit the buns with a sharp knife at the side. Lower the temperature to 180°C (350°F/gas mark 4) and bake for a further 20 minutes, until crisp. Cool on a wire rack.

5. Beat together all the ingredients for the filling. Spoon into a piping bag fitted with a 0.5cm (¼in) plain nozzle. Fill the buns through the slit in the side and place on a serving plate.

6. Spread a tiny amount of MARMITE on the top of each bun and sprinkle with chopped parsley just before serving.

Makes 16-20

Serve the buns fairly soon after filling to prevent the pastry becoming too soft.

LEFT Spanakopitta   RIGHT Cheese and Cucumber Mousse   BOTTOM Marinated Mushroom Salad

PICNICS & PACKED LUNCHES

MEDITERRANEAN STUFFED TOMATOES

Take a Mediterranean salad on your picnic - all tucked inside a beef tomato, for ease of transport!

Preparation time: 15 minutes

**4 LARGE BEEF TOMATOES
50G (2OZ) FRESH BREADCRUMBS
1 TBSP CHOPPED FRESH BASIL (OR 1 TSP DRIED)
1 TSP MARMITE YEAST EXTRACT
1 SMALL ONION, VERY FINELY CHOPPED
75-125G (3-4OZ) MOZZARELLA CHEESE, GRATED
1 SMALL AVOCADO, FINELY CHOPPED
2 TSP LEMON JUICE
6 BLACK OLIVES, PITTED AND CHOPPED
FRESHLY GROUND BLACK PEPPER
OLIVES AND FRESH BASIL TO GARNISH
(OPTIONAL)**

1. Cut the tops from the tomatoes - try to do a zig-zag cut if possible. Carefully scoop out the insides, discard the tops and cores and place the remaining seeds in a bowl.

2. Mix the breadcrumbs with the tomato, basil, MARMITE and onion. If the Mozzarella is in long strands, reserve a few and chop the others into smaller pieces before adding to the mixture. Toss the avocado in the lemon juice and add it with the chopped olives. Season to taste with black pepper.

3. Fill the tomatoes carefully with the mixture. Place a little Mozzarella on top of each and garnish with olives and basil.

Serves 4

MARINATED MUSHROOM SALAD

Preparation time: 10 minutes
Chilling time: 2 hours

**225G (8OZ) CHESTNUT MUSHROOMS, SLICED
2 CLOVES GARLIC, CRUSHED
3 TBSP CHOPPED FRESH PARSLEY
FRESHLY GROUND BLACK PEPPER
1 TSP MARMITE YEAST EXTRACT
200ML (7 FL OZ) EXTRA VIRGIN OLIVE OIL**

1. Mix the mushrooms with the garlic, parsley and pepper. In a small bowl, stir the MARMITE into the olive oil until it starts to blend, then pour over the mushrooms, stirring lightly.

2. Chill the salad for about 2 hours, stirring from time to time. Season to taste, if necessary, before serving.

Serves 4

Extra virgin olive oil is green in colour and rich in flavour. It is the least refined of the olive oils and is best used only in salads or dishes that do not require cooking, otherwise the flavour is wasted.

JUST LIKE WINE AND CHEESE, OLIVE OILS HAVE INDIVIDUAL CHARACTERISTICS OF AROMA AND COLOUR DEPENDING ON THE AREA WHERE THEY ARE PRODUCED.

SPANAKOPITTA

This traditional Greek dish can be made as one large pie or as individual rolls for packed lunches.

Preparation time: 25 minutes
Cooking time: 30 minutes

FILLING:

900G (2LB) FROZEN SPINACH,
COOKED, CHOPPED AND DRAINED
200G (7OZ) CREAM CHEESE
2 CLOVES GARLIC, CRUSHED
1TSP FRESHLY GRATED NUTMEG
(OR ½TSP GROUND)
1TBSP (3TSP) MARMITE YEAST EXTRACT
200G (7OZ) FETA CHEESE,
CUT INTO SMALL CUBES
FRESHLY GROUND BLACK PEPPER

PASTRY:

8-12 SHEETS FILO PASTRY (DEPENDING ON SIZE),
DEFROSTED
50G (2OZ) BUTTER, MELTED

Preheat oven to 200°C (400°F/gas mark 6)

1. Mix together all the ingredients for the filling, seasoning with plenty of black pepper. Add the spinach and Feta cheese last for easiest mixing.

2. Line a 25cm (10in) flan dish with half the filo pastry, brushing each sheet with melted butter to keep it moist. Allow the edges to overlap the dish.

3. Pile all the filling into the dish, press down firmly, and top the pie with the remaining pastry, brushing the layers with butter. Seal the edges together and trim. Score the top of the pie with a sharp knife.

4. Bake in the oven for 30 minutes, until the pastry is crisp, flaky and browned. Allow to cool and serve warm or cold.

Serves 4-6, or makes 12 rolls

If you make individual rolls they will require only half the amount of filling and just 15-20 minutes cooking. Fold the pastry as for the Crunchy Vegetable Rolls (page 13).

CHEESE AND CUCUMBER MOUSSE

If there is any of this mousse left over, it makes a wonderful sandwich filling. Refrigerate it and eat the next day.

Preparation time: 10 minutes
Chilling time: 2 hours

2TSP MARMITE YEAST EXTRACT
150ML (¼ PINT) BOILING WATER
24G (0.85OZ) PACKET ASPIC POWDER
225G (8OZ) CHEDDAR
OR RED LEICESTER CHEESE, GRATED
½ CUCUMBER, GRATED AND SQUEEZED DRY
450G (1LB) POT NATURAL YOGURT
3TBSP MAYONNAISE
1TSP WHOLEGRAIN MUSTARD
1TBSP CHOPPED FRESH MIXED HERBS
(OR 1TSP DRIED)
SALT AND FRESHLY GROUND BLACK PEPPER

1. Dissolve the MARMITE in the boiling water, add the aspic powder and stir well. Add sufficient cold water to make up to 300ml (½ pint). Allow to cool.

2. In a bowl, mix together the remaining ingredients. Add the cooled aspic liquid and mix thoroughly. Season to taste.

3. Rinse an 18cm (7in) ring mould with cold water - or set the mousse in a 1.5 litre (2½ pint) soufflé dish. Spoon in the mixture and chill in the fridge for 2 hours, or until set.

4. Turn the mousse out of the ring mould, if used, onto a serving plate. Serve with a tomato and onion salad.

Serves 6

For a change you can grate two courgettes into the mousse in place of the cucumber.

Metal ring moulds should be held in a bowl of hot water for 5-10 seconds to loosen the mousse before turning out onto a serving plate.

BRUSHING GLYCERINE ON THE INSIDE OF THE FREEZER AFTER DEFROSTING MAKES THE JOB EASIER AND FASTER NEXT TIME. THE BUILD UP OF ICE WILL SIMPLY FALL OFF.

TRY TO USE VEGETABLES WITHOUT PEELING. THIS RETAINS MAXIMUM FIBRE AND NUTRIENTS BUT DOES MEAN YOU HAVE TO WASH THEM VERY WELL BEFORE USE.

CHEESE AND NUT PÂTÉ

This pâté can be prepared very quickly. It travels well and is best eaten with fresh crusty bread.

Preparation time: 10 minutes
Chilling time: 1 hour

200G (7OZ) CREAM CHEESE
1 TSP MARMITE YEAST EXTRACT
1 SMALL ONION, VERY FINELY CHOPPED
2 STICKS CELERY, VERY FINELY CHOPPED
1/2 TSP PAPRIKA
125G (4OZ) MEDIUM CHEDDAR
OR RED LEICESTER CHEESE, GRATED
50G (2OZ) PISTACHIO KERNELS,
ROUGHLY CHOPPED
50G (2OZ) SALTED PEANUTS OR CASHEWS,
ROUGHLY CHOPPED
25G (1OZ) GLACÉ GINGER, FINELY CHOPPED
1 TBSP CHOPPED FRESH PARSLEY
(OR 1 TSP DRIED)
SALT AND FRESHLY GROUND BLACK PEPPER

1. In a bowl, beat the cream cheese until soft with the MARMITE. Add the onion, celery and paprika, and mix well.

2. Stir in the cheese and nuts, then add the ginger and parsley. Season to taste, if necessary.

3. Pile the pâté into a small serving dish or a plastic picnic dish. Cover and chill for 1 hour.

Serves 6-8

If you are not keen on raw onion, cook it in a little olive oil until soft, before adding it to the cream cheese.

If you are making this for an impromptu picnic and there is no time to chill it at home, pack it with an ice-pack until required.

PICNIC PLAIT

This is easy to slice and travels well, whether in a smart picnic box or knapsack!

Preparation time: 20 minutes
Cooking time: 30-35 minutes

450G (1 LB) PORK SAUSAGEMEAT
1 TBSP (3 TSP) MARMITE YEAST EXTRACT
1 TBSP TOMATO PURÉE
1 ONION, FINELY CHOPPED
1 GREEN PEPPER,
DE-SEEDED AND FINELY CHOPPED
SALT AND FRESHLY GROUND BLACK PEPPER
350G (12OZ) PACKET FROZEN PUFF PASTRY,
THAWED
50G (2OZ) CHEDDAR CHEESE, GRATED
1 EGG, BEATEN

Preheat oven to 220°C (425°F/gas mark 7)

1. Mix the sausagemeat in a bowl with the MARMITE and tomato purée. Add the onion, pepper and seasonings.

2. Roll the pastry into a rectangle 40cm x 30cm (16in x 12in). Pile the sausagemeat down the centre, then scatter the cheese over the meat. Brush the exposed pastry with the egg, and cut into diagonal strips, about 2cm (3/4in) wide, to plait over the filling.

3. Fold the top and bottom ends of the pastry over the sausagemeat, then fold the strips over to form a plait. Brush the pastry with beaten egg.

4. Bake in the oven for 30-35 minutes. Cool completely on a wire rack, then slice and use as required.

Serves 4-6

If you are good at making plaits, scatter the cheese over the sausagemeat before folding the pastry over. If not, use the cheese to hide the evidence, by scattering it over the pastry at the end of point 3.

DRESS SALAD LEAVES AT THE LAST MOMENT TO PREVENT THEM GOING LIMP AND SOGGY. SALADS MADE WITH PULSES, POTATOES, RICE OR PASTA, HOWEVER, SHOULD BE DRESSED WHILE THE INGREDIENTS ARE STILL WARM SO THAT THEY ABSORB MAXIMUM FLAVOUR.

PREPARED SALADS WILL LOSE SOME OF THEIR FLAVOUR IF SERVED TOO COLD, SO TAKE THEM OUT OF THE FRIDGE 20 MINUTES BEFORE EATING.

WALNUT AND BROCCOLI QUICHE

Preparation time: 20 minutes
Cooking time: 40-45 minutes

PASTRY:

175G (6OZ) WHOLEWHEAT PLAIN FLOUR
75G (3OZ) BUTTER OR MARGARINE
1 TSP MARMITE YEAST EXTRACT
WARM WATER TO MIX

FILLING:

1 ONION, FINELY CHOPPED
1 TBSP VEGETABLE OIL
225G (8OZ) BROCCOLI FLORETS,
CUT INTO SMALL PIECES
1 TSP MARMITE YEAST EXTRACT
125G (4OZ) WALNUT PIECES
75G (3OZ) RED LEICESTER CHEESE, GRATED
1 TSP FRESHLY GRATED NUTMEG
(OR 1/2 TSP GROUND NUTMEG)
225G (8OZ) FROMAGE FRAIS
300ML (1/2 PINT) MILK
3 EGGS, BEATEN

Preheat oven to 200°C (400°F/gas mark 6)

1. Prepare the pastry - rub the butter or margarine into the flour until the mixture resembles fine breadcrumbs. Stir in the MARMITE, then mix the pastry to a manageable dough using warm water. Lightly knead on a floured surface, then roll out and use to line a deep, 20cm (8in) loose-bottomed flan tin.

2. Cook the onion in the oil until soft. Remove the pan from the heat, add the broccoli and stir in the MARMITE. Transfer the vegetables to the pastry case using a slotted spoon.

3. Add the walnuts, then the cheese and sprinkle on the nutmeg. Beat the fromage frais with the milk and eggs and pour into the flan case.

4. Bake for 10 minutes, then lower the temperature to 180°C (350°F/gas mark 4) for a further 30-35 minutes, until the quiche is set and golden brown.

5. Cool slightly and serve, or chill completely.

Serves 4-6

I always cook quiches in metal tins to ensure satisfactory results with the pastry. Start in a hot oven to get the pastry cooking, then lower the temperature to prevent the filling curdling. Never cut a quiche when it is hot - it makes the filling separate and become watery.

CHICKEN ALLSPICE

In hot weather a spicy dish can be most refreshing. This recipe combines a traditional hot weather favourite, the salad, with a spicy flavour of the Mediterranean.

Preparation time: 15 minutes
Cooking time: 25 minutes
Cooling time: 30-45 minutes
Chilling time: 1-2 hours

2 TBSP OLIVE OIL
1 LARGE ONION, FINELY SLICED
1 MEDIUM AUBERGINE,
HALVED AND FINELY SLICED
1 CLOVE GARLIC, CRUSHED
2 TSP GROUND CUMIN
1 TSP GROUND ALLSPICE
1 TBSP POPPY SEEDS
1 TSP MARMITE YEAST EXTRACT
400G (14OZ) CAN CHOPPED TOMATOES
400G (14OZ) CAN ARTICHOKE HEARTS,
DRAINED AND HALVED
450G (1LB) COOKED CHICKEN MEAT, DICED
SALT AND FRESHLY GROUND BLACK PEPPER
RAW SPINACH AND LETTUCE HEARTS
CHOPPED FRESH MIXED HERBS FOR GARNISH

1. Heat the oil in a large pan, add the onion, aubergine, garlic, spices and poppy seeds and cook slowly for about 4-5 minutes, covered, until the vegetables are soft.

2. Add the MARMITE and tomatoes. Bring to the boil and simmer, uncovered, for 10-15 minutes, until slightly reduced and thickened. Add the artichoke hearts, then leave to cool for 30-45 minutes.

3. Add the chicken. Season the sauce to taste, then transfer to a serving dish or picnic box, lined with raw spinach and lettuce hearts. Chill for 1-2 hours.

4. Garnish with herbs.

Serves 4

Serve with pitta breads or Italian ciabatta bread. (See Ciabatta Loaf Sandwiches, page 56.)

READY-GROUND SPICES QUICKLY LOSE THEIR FLAVOUR. FOR BEST RESULTS, PREPARE YOUR OWN - JUST BEFORE YOU NEED THEM - USING A COFFEE GRINDER.

Top Walnut and Broccoli Quiche   Centre Picnic Plait   Bottom Chicken Allspice

SUPER SANDWICHES

SAVOURY SCONE ROUNDS

Preparation time: 10 minutes
Cooking time: 25-30 minutes

450G (1LB) SELF-RAISING FLOUR
75G (3OZ) BUTTER OR MARGARINE
2TSP MARMITE YEAST EXTRACT
1TSP MUSTARD POWDER
PINCH SALT
125G (4OZ) CHEDDAR CHEESE, GRATED
300ML (½ PINT) MILK

Preheat oven to 220°C (425°F/gas mark 7)

1. Rub the butter or margarine into the flour until the mixture resembles fine breadcrumbs. Stir in the MARMITE, mustard, salt and cheese, and mix to a soft manageable dough with the milk.

2. Turn out onto a floured surface and knead the dough lightly. Divide the mixture in half and shape into two rounds, about 2.5cm (1in) thick. Place on a lightly greased baking sheet and, using a sharp knife, score each round into eight portions.

3. Bake in the oven for 25-30 minutes, until browned and firm. Cool on a wire rack, then serve buttered with MARMITE, cheese, peanut butter or other savoury spreads.

Makes 16 pieces

HAPSBURGS

We usually think of open sandwiches as being Danish, but these combine some favourite German foods on tasty German bread.

Preparation time: 10 minutes
Cooking time: 5 minutes

4 SLICES OF PUMPERNICKEL OR GERMAN RYE BREAD
MARMITE YEAST EXTRACT TO TASTE
4 FRANKFURTERS
125-175G (4-6OZ) QUARK OR FROMAGE FRAIS
4TBSP POTATO SALAD
SLICED DILL CUCUMBERS
1TBSP CHOPPED FRESH DILL OR PARSLEY

1. Spread the pumpernickel or rye bread with MARMITE.

2. Heat the frankfurters as directed on the pack, and slice.

3. Spread the bread with quark or fromage frais and top with the chopped frankfurters. Add the potato salad, then garnish with the dill cucumber slices and the chopped dill or parsley. Serve immediately.

Serves 4

TRY CHOPPED CHINESE LEAVES IN SANDWICHES INSTEAD OF LETTUCE. THEY HAVE A MORE INTERESTING FLAVOUR AND STAY CRISPER LONGER.

PLOUGHMAN'S LUNCH BREAD

Bread-making is now comparatively quick using fast-acting yeast. Making your own bread enables you to experiment with all kinds of different flavours.

Preparation time: 15 minutes
Proving time: 1 hour
Cooking time: 45 minutes

7G (¼OZ) SACHET FAST-ACTING DRIED YEAST
1KG (2¼LB) MALTED BROWN FLOUR
1 ONION, VERY FINELY SLICED OR CHOPPED
2TSP MARMITE YEAST EXTRACT
2TSP SALT
150G (5OZ) CHEDDAR CHEESE, GRATED
300ML (½ PINT) BEER
300ML (½ PINT) TEPID WATER (APPROX)
VEGETABLE OIL

1. In a large bowl, add the yeast to the flour; then stir in the onion, MARMITE, salt and most of the cheese. Make a well in the centre of the flour, then pour in the beer and most of the water, mixing as you do so.

2. Mix to a soft but manageable dough, adding more water if required. Turn onto a floured surface and knead thoroughly until the dough is smooth - this may take five minutes or more.

3. Lightly oil two 450g (1lb) loaf tins. Cut the dough into two, shape each piece and place in a tin. Cover with a damp cloth and leave in a warm place for about 1 hour, until the dough has doubled in size.

4. Scatter the remaining cheese over the loaves. Place them in a cold oven, turn on to 220°C (425°F/gas mark 7) and cook from cold for 45 minutes.

5. Turn the loaves out of the tins and tap them on the bottom - if cooked they will sound hollow. If necessary return the loaves to the oven without the tins for an extra 5 minutes. Cool on a wire rack.

Makes 2 large loaves

SOMERSET LOAF

A tealoaf based on a scone mix. It has an interesting texture and makes lovely sandwiches.

Preparation time: 15 minutes
Cooking time: 35-45 minutes

450G (1LB) SELF-RAISING FLOUR, WHOLEMEAL OR WHITE
½TSP MUSTARD POWDER
125G (4OZ) CHEDDAR CHEESE, GRATED
225G (8OZ) COTTAGE CHEESE
125G (4OZ) PEANUTS, SALTED OR PLAIN, CHOPPED
1TBSP CHOPPED FRESH CHIVES (OR 1TSP DRIED)
1TSP MARMITE YEAST EXTRACT
2 EGGS, BEATEN
300ML (½ PINT) MILK (APPROX)

Preheat oven to 190°C (375°F/gas mark 5)

1. Lightly grease a 900g (2lb) loaf tin.

2. Place the flour in a bowl with the mustard powder and stir in the Cheddar cheese. Stir in the cottage cheese and peanuts with the chopped chives.

3. Combine the MARMITE with the beaten eggs and add to the bowl with most of the milk. Mix to a stiff dropping consistency, adding more milk if necessary.

4. Turn the mixture into the prepared tin, smooth the top and make a slight well in the centre of the mixture. Bake in the oven for 35-45 minutes, until golden brown and a skewer inserted into the centre of the loaf comes out clean.

5. Remove from the tin and cool on a wire rack.

Makes 1 loaf

This loaf keeps well for 2-3 days. It is very good toasted, spread with MARMITE and topped with cottage cheese.

COAT PIECES OF FOOD IN SEASONED FLOUR QUICKLY AND WITH MINIMUM MESS BY PUTTING THE FLOUR AND THE FOOD IN A POLYTHENE BAG AND SHAKING.

THE CUSTOM OF CUTTING A CROSS IN THE TOP OF A LOAF OF BREAD ORIGINATES IN THE SUPERSTITION THAT THIS LET THE DEVIL OUT OF THE LOAF.

TOP Somerset Loaf CENTRE Chick Pea Naandwich BOTTOM Hapsburgs

TOP Ploughman's Lunch Bread   CENTRE Ciabatta Loaf Sandwiches   BOTTOM Bronx Buster

CHICK PEA NAANDWICH

This open sandwich uses a curried chick pea topping on a naan bread base. Filling, spicy and delicious.

Preparation time: 10 minutes
Cooking time: 10 minutes

1 ONION, FINELY CHOPPED
1 TBSP VEGETABLE OIL
1 TBSP MILD CURRY PASTE
1 TSP MARMITE YEAST EXTRACT
400G (14OZ) CAN CHICK PEAS
(OR BUTTER BEANS), DRAINED
2 NAAN BREADS
BUTTER (OPTIONAL)
150G (5OZ) NATURAL YOGURT
(PREFERABLY SET)
2 TBSP MANGO CHUTNEY
OR OTHER PICKLE OF YOUR CHOICE
1 TOMATO, SLICED
1 TBSP CHOPPED FRESH CORIANDER (OPTIONAL)

1. Cook the onion in the oil for 2-3 minutes, until soft. Add the curry paste and cook for a further 1-2 minutes, then add the MARMITE and chick peas or beans. Cook gently for 5-10 minutes.

2. Preheat the grill. Cook the naans for 1-2 minutes on each side, until well puffed and brown.

3. Spread with butter, if required, and top with the chick peas. Spoon the yogurt over and add chutney to taste.

4. Garnish the naans with the sliced tomato and sprinkle with coriander before serving immediately.

Serves 2-4

For a more substantial sandwich, cook some aubergines, courgettes or mushrooms with the onions, before adding the chick peas.

COOKED PULSES WILL KEEP IN THE REFRIGERATOR FOR SEVERAL DAYS, SO SAVE TIME AND ENERGY BY PREPARING THEM IN BULK. THEY ALSO FREEZE WELL.

BASIL WITH TOMATOES IN A SALAD OR PASTA DISH IS A CLASSIC TASTE COMBINATION. BASIL ALSO GOES WELL WITH EGGS, IN POTATO SALAD AND IN RICE-BASED SALADS.

CIABATTA LOAF SANDWICHES

Ciabatta is an Italian-style speciality bread made with olive oil. Available in most supermarkets, it is easier to make into sandwiches if it is sliced lengthways rather than in the conventional way.

Preparation time: 10 minutes
Cooking time: 5 minutes

1 CIABATTA LOAF
MARMITE YEAST EXTRACT TO TASTE
4 CRISP LETTUCE LEAVES, SHREDDED
175G (6OZ) SMOKED GOATS' CHEESE
(EG BURNDELL), GRATED;
OR 4 SMALL GOATS' CHEESES IN OLIVE OIL
1 TBSP EXTRA VIRGIN OLIVE OIL
2 LARGE RIPE TOMATOES, SLICED
1 RIPE AVOCADO, PEELED AND SLICED
6 OLIVES, PITTED AND HALVED

Preheat oven to 180°C (350°F/gas mark 4)

1. Place the bread in the oven to heat through for 5 minutes.

2. Split the ciabatta lengthways and spread the base thinly with MARMITE. Line with lettuce.

3. Add the grated cheese and drizzle a little olive oil over, or spread the softer goats' cheese in oil over the lettuce and drizzle with a little of the oil from the cheeses.

4. Top with tomatoes, avocado and olives, and place the top of the loaf over the filling. Cut into four equal portions, and serve.

Serves 4

TO MAKE SAVOURY RUSKS, CUT SLICES OF BREAD INTO FINGERS AND SPREAD VERY THINLY WITH **MARMITE** YEAST EXTRACT. PLACE ON A BAKING SHEET AND DRY OUT AT 130°C (250°F/GAS MARK 1/2) FOR 2 1/2 HOURS. STORE IN AN AIRTIGHT TIN.

BRONX BUSTER

This American sandwich is a complete meal.

Preparation time: 10 minutes
Cooking time: 5 minutes

4 ONION BAGELS OR CRISPY ROLLS
2 TBSP MAYONNAISE
1 TSP MARMITE YEAST EXTRACT
1 TBSP MILD GERMAN OR HONEY MUSTARD
125G (4OZ) CREAM CHEESE, BEATEN
8 SLICES ITALIAN SALAMI
2 TOMATOES, SLICED
2 TBSP CHOPPED (OR SLICED) RAW PEPPERS

Preheat oven to 180°C (350°F/gas mark 4)

1. Heat the bagels for 4-5 minutes. If using crusty rolls they will not require heating.

2. Mix together the mayonnaise and MARMITE. Split the bagels and spread the base with the savoury mayonnaise and the lid with mustard.

3. Spread generously with cream cheese and top with a layer of salami. Then add the tomato slices and chopped peppers.

4. Close the bagels or rolls, and serve.

Serves 4

Onion bagels are a traditional Jewish-American bread. They are available in most supermarkets.

JARLSBERG TORPEDOES

Jarlsberg is a Norwegian cheese, similar to Emmenthal but slightly sweeter. It has become very popular in recent years.

Preparation time: 10 minutes
Cooking time: 4 minutes

6 RASHERS BACK BACON, CHOPPED
4 TORPEDO ROLLS, SOFT OR CRUSTY
BUTTER
MARMITE YEAST EXTRACT TO TASTE
4 LARGE OR 8 SMALL SLICES JARLSBERG CHEESE
16 GREEN SEEDLESS GRAPES, HALVED

1. Cook the bacon in a small frying pan for 3-4 minutes, until browned.

2. Split the rolls and spread with butter and MARMITE. Top with the Jarlsberg, grapes and bacon. Close and serve immediately.

Makes 4

The bacon can be allowed to cool completely and then be served cold in the rolls.

TO GIVE SANDWICHES A SAVOURY LIFT, MIX A LITTLE MARMITE YEAST EXTRACT INTO THE BUTTER OR MARGARINE FOR SPREADING.

MARMITE YEAST EXTRACT IS A VALUABLE SOURCE OF FIVE OF THE B GROUP VITAMINS, PARTICULARLY RIBOFLAVIN AND NIACIN, WHICH ARE ESSENTIAL FOR ENERGY AND FOR PROMOTING NORMAL GROWTH, HEALTHY SKIN AND GENERAL FITNESS.

MASH A BANANA WITH A LITTLE MARMITE YEAST EXTRACT. SPREAD THE MIXTURE ON BUTTERED BROWN BREAD. CUT INTO FINGERS AND SERVE AS A DELICIOUS TEATIME TREAT FOR CHILDREN.

BREAD IS EASIER TO SLICE IF YOU PUT IT IN THE FRIDGE FOR ABOUT HALF AN HOUR FIRST, AND USE A LONG-BLADED SERRATED KNIFE.

CHILDREN'S PARTY FOOD

JUNIOR GARLIC BREAD

Popular with children of all ages, the flavour of garlic bread is enhanced by the addition of MARMITE.

Preparation time: 10 minutes
Cooking time: 15-20 minutes

1 SMALL FRENCH STICK OR BÂTON
1 CLOVE GARLIC, CRUSHED
1 TSP MARMITE YEAST EXTRACT
125G (4OZ) SOFTENED BUTTER

Preheat oven to 200°C (400°F/gas mark 6)

1. Cut the bread, but do not quite separate the slices.

2. Beat the garlic and MARMITE into the butter. Spread liberally on one side of each cut in the bread.

3. Wrap the bread in foil and bake for 15-20 minutes. Unwrap, break the slices apart and serve immediately.

Makes 1 small loaf

Ⓥ

EGGY ANIMALS

MARMITE complements the flavour of egg mayonnaise beautifully, making it less rich. Cut the sandwiches into animal shapes for a special party centrepiece.

Preparation time: 15 minutes

10 SLICES SANDWICH BREAD,
WHITE OR WHOLEWHEAT
BUTTER OR MARGARINE FOR SPREADING
MARMITE YEAST EXTRACT TO TASTE
6 EGGS, HARD-BOILED
6 TBSP MAYONNAISE OR SALAD CREAM
1 PUNNET CRESS

1. Spread the bread with butter or margarine and spread half the slices with MARMITE.

2. Peel the eggs and mash them with a fork, then bind together with mayonnaise or salad cream.

3. Spread the mixture on the bread, scatter the cress over and complete the sandwiches with the remaining bread. Remove the crusts.

4. Cut the sandwiches into shapes using animal-shaped cutters. Use MARMITE to make eyes, spots and stripes as appropriate, and arrange on a serving platter.

Makes up to 10 animals

Make a farmyard, zoo or jungle scene with watercress for grass, salad and raw vegetables for trees and bushes, and savoury snacks for houses etc.

CRUSH GARLIC ON A CLEAN SHEET OF GREASEPROOF OR
SILICON PAPER TO AVOID TAINTING YOUR CHOPPING BOARD.

TOP Pasta Boats   *LEFT* Sticks and Swirls   *RIGHT* Eggy Animals

PASTA BOATS

Try these pasta boats as an alternative to the more traditional bridge roll boats.

Preparation time: 25 minutes
Cooking time: 20 minutes
Cooling time: 30 minutes

SALT
VEGETABLE OIL
12 LARGE VENETIAN PASTA SHELLS
1 RIPE AVOCADO, PEELED AND CHOPPED
1 TBSP LEMON JUICE
1 RED PEPPER, DE-SEEDED AND FINELY CHOPPED
1 SMALL COURGETTE OR 1/2 CUCUMBER, FINELY CHOPPED
3 TBSP MAYONNAISE
1 TSP MARMITE YEAST EXTRACT
SHREDDED GREEN LETTUCE FOR SERVING
12 FLAG COCKTAIL STICKS FOR DECORATION

1. Bring a very large pan of water, with a little salt and oil, to the boil. Add the pasta shells, return to the boil and simmer for 15 minutes. Drain and rinse immediately with boiling water, then leave to cool.

2. Toss the avocado in the lemon juice in a bowl, then combine it with the pepper and courgette or cucumber.

3. Blend the mayonnaise with the MARMITE and stir into the prepared vegetables.

4. Pile the vegetables into the pasta shells, arranging the filled boats on a sea of shredded lettuce.

5. Use cocktail sticks with flags as sails.

Makes 12

♥

If you feel really artistic, make sails from slivers of cheese on sticks, topped with a cocktail onion.

STICKS AND SWIRLS

A MARMITE variation on cheese straws.

Preparation time: 15-25 minutes
Cooking time: 10-15 minutes

350G (12OZ) PREPARED PUFF PASTRY
BUTTER OR MARGARINE
MARMITE YEAST EXTRACT TO TASTE

Preheat oven to 220°C (425°F/gas mark 7)

1. Lightly grease a large baking sheet.

2. Roll out the pastry to a rectangle about 30cm x 40cm (12in x 16in), with the longest edge nearest you. Trim the edges straight, and spread the pastry very thinly with butter or margarine. Then spread with MARMITE.

3. Cut the pastry in half horizontally, along the edge in front of you.

4. Cut half the pastry into long strips about 2cm (3/4 in) wide. Carefully twist the straws once and place them on the baking sheet - there should be a stripe of MARMITE spiralling around each straw.

5. Cut the remaining pastry into slightly thinner strips. Roll up very loosely into swirls, allowing room for the pastry to spread during cooking. Place on the baking sheet.

6. Bake in the oven for 10-15 minutes. Cool on a wire rack before serving.

Makes about 24

Although there is fat in the pastry you will need to butter it lightly to bind the swirls and to make the adhesion of the MARMITE easier. Use shortcrust pastry if you prefer, but cook at a slightly lower temperature: 200°C (400°F/gas mark 6).

Scatter a little Parmesan cheese over the shapes before baking, for a change.

TO MAKE CHILDREN'S PARTY SAUSAGES, MIX TOGETHER 1 TBSP (3 TSP) **MARMITE** YEAST EXTRACT AND 1 TBSP WATER IN A SMALL ROASTING TIN, AND COAT 24 CHIPOLATAS EVENLY. BAKE IN THE OVEN FOR 25 MINUTES ON 200°C (400°F/GAS MARK 6), TURNING AND BASTING ONCE OR TWICE. CUT EACH SAUSAGE IN TWO AND SERVE ON COCKTAIL STICKS.

A ROASTING PAN FILLED WITH HOT WATER IN THE BOTTOM OF THE OVEN WILL HELP PUFF PASTRY TO RISE AND BECOME CRISP.

SAVOURY PUMPKIN SEEDS

These will be really popular with young guests, and make a welcome change from crisps.

Preparation time: 5 minutes
Cooking time: 5 minutes

1 TBSP (3 TSP) **MARMITE** YEAST EXTRACT
1 TBSP BOILING WATER
150G (5OZ) PUMPKIN SEEDS

1. Dissolve the MARMITE in the boiling water. Place the pumpkin seeds in the grill pan, pour the MARMITE liquid over and toss them until well coated.

2. Cook under a preheated grill for 4-5 minutes, stirring occasionally, until toasted.

3. Allow to cool, then separate the seeds with your fingers or a fork, leaving them in small clumps.

4. Store in an air-tight jar if the seeds are not going to be used immediately.

Sunflower seeds can also be used for this recipe.

PARTY PANCAKES

Preparation time: 30 minutes
Cooking time: 20 minutes

PANCAKES:
1 EGG
300ML (½ PINT) MILK
1 TSP **MARMITE** YEAST EXTRACT
125G (4OZ) PLAIN FLOUR
VEGETABLE OIL

FILLING:
325G (12OZ) CAN SWEETCORN KERNELS, DRAINED
125G (4OZ) MIXED CHOPPED NUTS
½ TSP **MARMITE** YEAST EXTRACT
125G (4OZ) EDAM CHEESE, CUT INTO THIN WAFERS

TOPPING:
SMALL PACKET POTATO CRISPS, CRUSHED (ANY FLAVOUR)
SPRIGS OF PARSLEY

Preheat the oven to 190°C (375°F/gas mark 5)

1. To prepare the pancakes, place the egg, milk and MARMITE in a liquidiser or food processor and blend together. While the blades are running, gradually add the flour and whisk until thoroughly blended. (The batter may also be made by placing the egg, MARMITE and flour in a bowl and beating together, gradually whisking in the milk.)

2. Use the mixture to make 10 pancakes in a small omelette pan. Lightly oil the pan between each pancake. Stack the pancakes between sheets of kitchen paper.

3. Mix together all the ingredients for the filling (the cheese will melt and bind the filling in the oven).

4. Divide the filling between the pancakes, roll them up and place in a single layer in a lightly greased ovenproof dish. Bake for 20 minutes.

5. Garnish the pancakes with the crushed crisps and parsley sprigs. Serve immediately.

Makes 10

TO MAKE A TRIPLE-DECKER BEEFBURGER, MAKE TWO HORIZONTAL SLITS IN A BAP, AND SPREAD EACH LAYER WITH **MARMITE** YEAST EXTRACT. PUT THE COOKED BURGER AND SOME ONION RINGS IN THE LOWER CAVITY AND FILL THE OTHER WITH LETTUCE, SLICES OF CHEDDAR CHEESE AND TOMATO – AND YOUR CHOICE OF RELISH.

MARMITE YEAST EXTRACT ADDED TO BATTERS FOR PANCAKES ENHANCES THE FLAVOUR OF THE FILLING. THESE PANCAKES CAN BE MADE IN BULK, LAYERED IN GREASEPROOF PAPER AND FROZEN.

TOP LEFT Tuna and Tomato Flan   TOP RIGHT Savoury Pumpkin Seeds   CENTRE Chequer Board   BOTTOM Party Pancakes

TUNA AND TOMATO FLAN

Preparation time: 20 minutes
Cooking time: 35-45 minutes

225G (8OZ) PREPARED PUFF PASTRY
40G (1½OZ) BUTTER OR MARGARINE
40G (1½OZ) PLAIN FLOUR
300ML (½ PINT) MILK
185G (6½OZ) CAN TUNA IN BRINE, DRAINED
1 TSP MARMITE YEAST EXTRACT
3 TOMATOES, SLICED
50G (2OZ) CHEDDAR CHEESE, GRATED

Preheat oven to 200°C (400°F/gas mark 6)

1. Roll out the pastry and use to line a deep, 20cm (8in) metal flan tin.

2. To prepare the white sauce, melt the butter or margarine in a saucepan, stir in the flour and cook for 30 seconds, without browning, over a low heat. Add the milk gradually and bring to the boil, stirring all the time. Remove from the heat.

3. Stir the tuna and MARMITE into the sauce, then spoon it into the pastry case. Top with the sliced tomatoes and scatter the cheese over.

4. Bake in the oven for 35-45 minutes. Serve hot or cold.

Serves 6

CHEQUER BOARD

This is very simple to do, looks great and always gets eaten up.

Preparation time: 15 minutes

8 SLICES WHOLEWHEAT SANDWICH BREAD
8 SLICES WHITE SANDWICH BREAD
BUTTER OR MARGARINE FOR SPREADING
MARMITE YEAST EXTRACT TO TASTE

FILLINGS:
CREAM CHEESE AND CUCUMBER
SARDINES OR PILCHARDS IN TOMATO SAUCE
PEANUT BUTTER WITH GRATED CARROT

1. Spread the bread with butter or margarine and spread half the slices with MARMITE. Choose a filling and complete the sandwiches so each is made from one slice of white bread and one of wholewheat. Remove the crusts.

2. Cut each sandwich into four squares.

3. Arrange the sandwiches on a platter or tray to resemble a chequer board.

Makes 16 small sandwiches

Don't be too generous with the fillings in case they leak over the bread and spoil the pattern.

SCRAMBLED EGGS WILL BE FLUFFIER IF A LITTLE WATER IS ADDED BEFORE COOKING. DO NOT OVERCOOK THEM OR THEY WILL SEPARATE AND BECOME WATERY.

MOST OF THE FLAVOUR OF PARSLEY IS FOUND IN THE STALKS. IF YOU ARE ONLY USING THE LEAVES, RETAIN THE STALKS TO FLAVOUR SOUPS AND STEWS, BUT REMOVE BEFORE SERVING.

IF A SAUCE GOES LUMPY BEFORE IT HAS COME TO THE BOIL YOU SHOULD BE ABLE TO RESCUE IT BY BEATING VIGOROUSLY WITH A WIRE WHISK. IF IT GOES LUMPY AFTER IT HAS BOILED, YOU WILL HAVE TO TRY PASSING IT THROUGH A FINE SIEVE OR USE A FOOD PROCESSOR OR BLENDER.

INDEX